Praise

Worship

And

The Spirit Of Prophecy

Fidel M. Donaldson

To: Colleen Morgan

God bless You

Shalom

Fidel M. Donaldson

03- 05- 18

Praise

Worship

And

The Spirit Of Prophecy

"And I fell at his feet to worship him. And he said unto me, See thou do it not: I am thy fellow servant, and of thy brethren that have the testimony of Jesus: worship God: for the testimony of Jesus is the spirit of prophecy." (*Revelation 19:10*)

Fidel M. Donaldson

Dedicated to true worshippers who worship the Father in Spirit and in truth!

Praise Worship and the Spirit of Prophecy by Fidel M. Donaldson
Copyright © 2013 Appeal Ministries

ISBN: 978-0-9827710-4-4
LCCN: 2013914714

Cover design by: Designs By Reign Flo Lee Von Nutall
Scripture quotations in this publication are from the King James Version of the Bible.

Printed in the United States of America

Acknowledgement

My heartfelt thanks to Minister Lurline Green, Dr. Tassel Daley Lee Von and Charlena Nutall for helping to birth out this book I bless God for my brother Patrice Donaldson a.k.a Lenky, and the Christian soldiers at Otisville FCI for their prayers and encouragement, and to all Christian soldiers behind the wall, keep worshipping King Jesus Yeshua: The Conquering Lion of the tribe of Judah. Agape Shalom to my wife for life Mrs. Paulette Donaldson a.k.a Mrs Cuty Cuty.

Table Of Contents

FOREWORD...Viii

PREFACE..x

PART ONE

Chapter 1 PRAISE 14

Chapter 2 PRAISE IS MY PLATFORM.................................21

Chapter 3 WORSHIP GOD...28

PART TWO

Chapter 4 A VOICE LIKE A TRUMPT...............................40

Chapter 5 SPIRIT AND TRUTH WORSHIP............................52

Chapter 6 THE SPIRIT OF PROPHECY................................64

PART THREE

Chapter 7 PROPHETIC MANIFESTATION...........................72

Chapter 8 YOUR SONS AND YOUR DAUGHTERS SHALL PROPHESY........82

Chapter 9 THE MINSTREL AND THE PROPHET.....................89

PART FOUR

Chapter 10 IS SAUL AMONG THE PROPHETS.......................99

Chapter 11 WORSHIP IS MY PROPHETIC WEAPON................106

Chapter 12 NEW TESTAMENT PROPHECY..........................113

PART FIVE

Chapter 13 THERE IS A PROPHETIC WORD IN YOUR BELLY.............131

Chapter 14 IT'S TIME TO PROPHESY................................141

Chapter 15 PROPHETIC PERFORMANCE.............................151

FOREWORD

The purpose and focus of our existence is glorifying God through our relationship with Him through praise and worship. As a person who has been exposed to different forms of praise and worship throughout my Christian walk, I often wondered what constitutes true praise and worship in church. Is it the music style or is it how the congregation responds emotionally during the praise service?

It is timely that Apostle Fidel Donaldson should explore the correlation between praise, worship and the Spirit of Prophecy. In this riveting book he shows us how in worship, we give God our undivided attention and respond to Him with extravagant praise. This offering of ourselves to God permeates every part of our existence and simply continues when we gather with other believers. That simply means that worship is not an event, but rather a lifestyle. Our worship flows out of an experience with and exposure to the love of God.

While we welcome the prophetic ministry (Acts 2:17-18; I Cor. 14:1, 3), the writer believes that the Bible is the infallible, unchanging Word of God and that all "words" must be measured against His absolute standard. Each chapter appeals to me as he uses scriptural evidence throughout his book from the word of God to show the correlation between praise, worship and the spirit of prophecy. He gives us insight about how the Bible has much to say about the many forms of worship and expose to the reader that not only does the Bible guide our expression of worship, but is also the primary tool that the Holy Spirit uses to teach us and build our faith.

Throughout each section the writer exposes the reader to how God speaks to us in His word and expressed that as believers we must be taught the scriptural dynamics of praise and worship and how they relate to individual and corporate prophecy. He reminds us how we must worship God with the truth about ourselves and Him, approaching Him as we are, and as He has revealed Himself to be while exposing the reader to several Hebrew words for praise.

As one who operates in the prophetic, the author also believes that God speaks to us prophetically. Prophecy is simply hearing God speak and communicating what He says in love and wisdom when it is needed and appropriate. Its primary purpose is "edification, encouragement and consolation" (I Corinthians 14:3). Prophecy is poured out in worship. He posits that there is a close relationship between worship and prophecy. (1 Chron. 25:1).

This captivating book guides the reader to understand that worship should flow from praise to intimacy with God because He is not a distant power, held at arms-length from us in awe, but a close and trusted friend, but more than that, a loving and kind father.

As you read this book and apply the contents to your personal worship experience, it will motivate you to better understand that "worship is not external but begins internally with a heart and mind that is yielded to God."

Lurline Green, M.A.

Child of God

Teacher, song writer, recording artist

Worship leader

Guidance Counselor

PREFACE

The correlation between praise, worship and the Spirit of prophecy is a dynamic subject. Prior to getting revelation on these topics and their connection, I never thought about the manner in which they were connected and their importance to every child of God. One day, while reading-of all books, *the book of Revelation*, the Holy Spirit enlightened the eyes of my understanding so I could understand the importance. As I expanded my study, I saw many other scriptures that confirmed the aforementioned connection.

When we praise and worship God individually or come together corporately on one accord in the unity of the Spirit, an atmosphere is created that is conducive to the voice of prophecy. Without true Spirit led praise and worship we will not be able to hear and discern the voice of God in the word spoken through His chosen vessels. Since the scriptures tell us that, *"the letter killeth but the Spirit gives life"* (*2 Corinthians 3:6*). We need the Spirit to give life to the word we preach, teach, and hear.

I believe there is a prophetic voice in every Spirit filled Christian that will be activated when there is Spirit and truth praise and worship. As believers we must be taught the scriptural dynamics of praise and worship and how they relate to individual and corporate prophecy. My thesis is this-God desires to speak prophetically to us and through us and He does it through the Holy Spirit and praise and worship is a key facilitator of this. It is essential that we learn to hear and discern the voice of God, and be confident to speak forth His prophetic word with confidence and boldness. You don't have to be a prophet to prophesy. If the Spirit of God is dwelling on the inside of you then He will speak prophetically to you and through you.

Whether in your private time of devotion or in a corporate service, God desires to commune with and to speak to and through us. We must have an expectation that when we enter the secret place through worship, a prophetic word will come forth. We should not shun prophecy because there has been excesses and abuse. Prophecy is a key component of the New Testament Church just as it was in the Old Testament. The Apostle Paul told the Church at Corinth, *"Wherefore, brethren, covet to prophesy, and forbid not to speak with tongues. Let all things be done decently and in order" (1 Corinthians 14:39-40).* The word covet there means to be zealous for something. As long as things are being done in decency and in order, every Christian should worship with an expectation of a release of the voice of prophesy through the Holy Spirit.

My prayer, my earnest expectation and desire is that as you read this book, the Holy Spirit will give you a greater understanding of the synthesis between praise, worship and the Spirit of prophecy which will activate the prophetic in you.

PART ONE

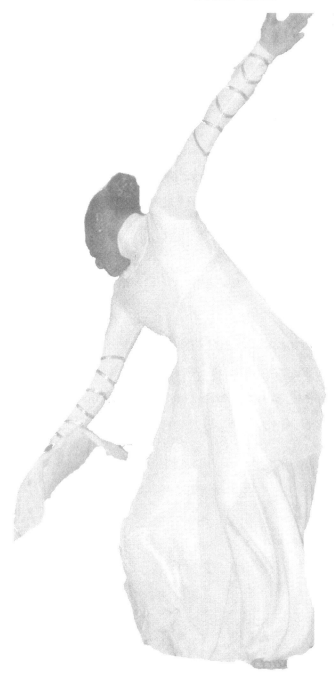

Fidel Donaldson

Praise Worship and the Spirit of Prophecy

Chapter 1
Praise

The Levitical Priesthood

My sister Janet has a prayer-line where intercessors gather to pray at 5a.m. There are individuals on the line who are dedicated to early Morning Prayer and they are consistently at their post. One morning, I was on with the team and shared an excerpt from this book on the Levites who were assigned to play on instruments before the Ark and also to sing. One of the sisters on the line shared how she had recently learned some things about the ministry of the Levite as she read the book of numbers; while she was sharing, the Holy Spirit revealed some things to me.

Aaron the first high priest and his sons were chosen from the tribe of Levi to minister before the Lord. The succession of the priesthood would come through the blood line of Aaron and if someone was not a descendent of Aaron he could not be a priest. The priesthood of Aaron or the Levitical priesthood was a temporary one, because Aaron and every high priest chosen from the tribe of Levi had to make atonement for their own sins when they went into the Holy of holies once a year.

The Judah Priesthood

With the advent of the ministry of the Lord Jesus came the establishment of a better and permanent priesthood. The book of Hebrews tells us that perfection did not come from the Levitical priesthood, because if it did there would not be further need for another priest to arise after the order of Melchisedec, and not be called after the order of Aaron. There was a paradigm shift in the priesthood when Jesus came, and the priesthood He instituted was not an exclusive one like the Levitical priesthood. In other words a person was not excluded because of their genealogy or their bloodline; the criterion for the new priesthood is salvation by grace through faith. The Bible declares, *"For it is evident that our Lord sprang out of Juda; of which tribe Moses spake nothing concerning priesthood"* (Hebrews 7:14).

Every blood washed redeemed child of God with the Holy Spirit is a member of the Judah priesthood, Judah means praise and God is raising up a sanctified priesthood of people to give Him praise honor and glory. It does not matter the type of family we came from, and we cannot be excluded because of natural blood lines because the blood of Jesus gives us the pedigree and the status needed to be a part of His priesthood.

Jesus is the Lion of the tribe of Juda and in the natural we know that the Lion is King and so it is in the spiritual. I was watching a program on public television recently; it was a documentary on lions. There was a picture shown of a lion walking along a trail. There were several Giraffes watching the lion and as soon as the lion came towards their direction they began to run. The giraffes were over ten feet tall but they understood the authority of the lion. You may be facing a situation that is larger than your natural ability to handle it, but when you praise the Lion of the tribe of Judah the giant will fall. The Juda priesthood must adopt the nature of the Lion of the tribe of Juda in our praise.

We must be bold and authoritative in praising our King. He came first as a Lamb to give us salvation, but He is currently reigning as the Lion King. Some Levites were chosen to play and sing before the presence of the Lord but the Juda priesthood is chosen to be a tabernacle or dwelling place for His presence. We are the offspring of the Lion of the tribe of Judah, so we do not need to fear the adversary who roars like a lion; he is not a lion he simply roars like a lion. Our high priest is the conquering Lion of the tribe of Judah. Hallelujah, bless His holy name!!!

Praise Worship and the Spirit of Prophecy

Judah Shall go up First

And the children of Israel arose, and went up to the house of God, and asked counsel of God, and said, which of us shall go up first to the battle against the children of Benjamin? And the LORD said, Judah shall go up first" (Judges 20:1-8). Judah means praise and praise must be first. It does not matter how great the battle, praise must go up first. When we assemble ourselves together, the praise and worship leader and the individuals on the instruments start with praise in-order to get us ready to enter a place of worship. Believers come together from differing backgrounds having different experience. Praise helps us to take the focus off people, places and things and to come together on one accord in thanking God. We can gain an understanding of the position of Judah by looking at the tabernacle and how the tribes were arranged around it. The tabernacle was the meeting place and it contained the Ark of God's presence; Moses was given specific instructions on the placement of the tribes.

The tribe of Judah was placed on the East side toward the rising of the Sun. An eastward direction in the scriptures is a Godly direction and confirms the fact that Judah praise must always be God-ward. The wise men that came to worship Jesus came from the East. When God created man He planted a garden eastward in Eden and there He placed man. Ezekiel saw the glory of the LORD going up from the midst of the city, and standing upon a mountain which is on the east side of the city. Judah was placed toward the rising of the Sun. The Sun gives light and heat to the earth, and the Son gives light and heat to the children of God. When Jesus returns it will be from the east. *"For as the lightning cometh out of the east, and shineth even unto the west; so shall also the coming of the Son of man be"* (Matthew 24:27).

Jesus Christ is worthy of praise as the Lion of the tribe of Judah. He has preeminence in all things. When it comes to the manifestation of the Spirit of prophecy, Judah must take the lead in praising the Lion King.

Fidel Donaldson

When I was a young Christian, I did not understand the difference between praise and worship although I heard both words on many occasions. My encounter with Jesus Christ that led to my salvation took place in an English prison and not in a church building. My first two years as a Christian was spent reading and studying the Bible on my own or with a few believers during Bible study in the prison. Reading the Bible taught me the importance of praise and worship but I needed some sound teaching on each subject. Not only did I not understand the distinction between praise and worship, but I also did not understand how they were connected to the moving of the Holy Spirit and the prophetic. When I was released and started to go to church, I began to learn more about praise and worship, but I did not get the increase until I heard someone say; *"We praise God for what He does but we worship Him for who He is!"* Once I began to study both subjects, I learned that praise is external and worship is internal. Praise can be undertaken by everyone, but true worship comes from an inner place of intimacy with God.

Praise sets the stage and gets the heart and mind ready to enter His presence with worship. God causes the sun to shine on the just and the unjust so everyone can praise Him. The psalmist declared, *"Let everything that hath breath praise the Lord, praise ye the Lord"* (Psalm 150:6). According to the psalmist, the criterion for praise is breathing. If we are breathing, we should praise God because He has done something for us in allowing us to have the breath of life, and without the breath of life everything ceases. The Hebrew word for praise used in *Psalm 150:6* is the word *halal* and when we examine the meaning of that word you realize it is not for the timid or the faint of heart. *Halal* means *to shine; to make a show, to boast;* and thus be *clamorously foolish; to celebrate* also *to stultify*. I must admit, before being filled with the Holy Ghost during a revival, I was one of those individuals who sat stoically in church during praise and worship observing those who dared to express themselves freely. *Halal* praise was out of the question back then because I was too concerned about how I looked in the eyes of others; in retrospect my

Praise Worship and the Spirit of Prophecy

concern should have been with how I looked in the eyes of God; more on the *halal* praise and other Hebrew words for praise later.

Like every other thing that pertains to God, we must look to the word of God to understand the different types of praise we are to offer up to Him. There are many Hebrew words for praise in the Bible and I believe these words give insight how the child of God should praise Him. The Bible teaches us to be thankful to Him for what He has done for us. If we are not thankful for what He has done we will not worship Him for who He is. If we do not like the fruit, then we will not care for the tree. Since blessings come down when the praises go up, we need to know the type of praises to send up to facilitate certain blessings.

The word praise is first used in the Bible in *Genesis 29:35:* It was used by Jacob's wife Leah when she was in a prolific child bearing season. *"And she conceived again, and bare a son: and she said, Now will I praise the LORD: therefore she called his name Judah; and left bearing."* The Hebrew word for praise there is *yadah* and it means; *to hold out the hands; to revere or worship with extended hands.* When God causes us to be fruitful in some area of our lives we should extend our hands and give Him *yadah* praise.

- The next word for praise is found in *Leviticus 19:24.* To understand the significance of *verse 24* we need to look at the previous verse. God told His people, *"And when ye shall come into the land, and shall have planted all manner of trees for food, then ye shall count the fruit thereof as uncircumcised: three years shall it be as uncircumcised unto you: it shall not be eaten."*
  Verse 24 states, *"But in the fourth year all the fruit thereof shall be holy to praise the LORD withal."* The word used for praise there is, *hilluwl* (pronounced *hil-lool*); *it speaks of rejoicing, a celebration of thanksgiving for harvest.* We actually get the word *halal* from this word (more on the word halal later). When God makes us fruitful, we shouldn't give Him a quick surface praise; we should spend time

rejoicing, and celebrating in His presence. Take note of the fact that both of those scriptures deal with praising God for allowing us to be fruitful.

- The next word for praise is found in *Deuteronomy 10:21*; Moses told the people, *"He is thy praise, and he is thy God, that hath done for thee these great and terrible things, which thine eyes have seen."* The Hebrew word for praise there is: *tehillah* and it means *laudation*, to *sing a hymn*. The word halal is also connected to this word. When we look and see all the great things the LORD has done for us, let us break forth in laudation and singing to give Him the *tehillah* praise.

- The next word for praise is found in *Judges 5:2, "Praise ye the LORD for the avenging of Israel, when the people willingly offered themselves."* The Hebrew word there is *barak* and it means to kneel to bless God as an act of adoration. Come let us bow down and worship, let kneel before the Lord God Almighty when He has avenged us of our enemies. The posture of kneeling is a wonderful way to show our adoration of our heavenly Father.

- In *1 Chronicles 16:4* my favorite type of praise is found. Concerning David the Bible declares, *"And he appointed certain of the Levites to minister before the ark of the LORD, and to record, and to thank and praise, the LORD God of Israel."* The word *halal* is used there, and as previously stated, it means *to shine, to make a show*, to *boast*, to *celebrate*, *rave* and to *stultify*. Only certain Levites were appointed to give God the *halal* praise because it is a radical praise. When David was dancing before the Lord with all his might he must have given God the *halal* praise. If you are one of those types of Levites, then get in God's presence and have a *halal* praise celebration.

Praise Worship and the Spirit of Prophecy

- *Psalm 7:17 declares, I will praise the LORD according to his righteousness: and will sing praise to the name of the LORD most high."* The Hebrew word *zamar* is used there and it

- means *to touch the strings or parts of a musical instrument, to make music, accompanied by the voice, hence to celebrate in song and music. To sing forth praises.* Meditate on God's righteousness and play and sing *zamar* praise to his wonderful name.

- Our next word for *praise* is found in *Psalm 50:23* where the psalmist declared, "*Whoso offereth praise glorifieth me: and to him that ordereth his conversation aright will I shew the salvation of God.*" The word used for praise there is *towdah*

- and it also means *to extend the hands in adoration but specifically to a choir of worshippers.* It also means *confession, sacrifice of praise, thanksgiving, offering.* This psalm was written by David when Nathan the prophet came to him after he had gone in to Bathsheba. When we sin we should confess, repent immediately and give God the *towdah* praise.

- The next word is found in *Daniel 2:23* where the Bible declares, "*I thank thee, and praise thee, O thou God of my fathers, who hast given me wisdom and might, and hast made known unto me now what we desired of thee: for thou hast now made known unto us the king's matter.*" Daniel used the word *shabach* there and it means to *adulate*, to *adore*. To address in a *loud tone*, to *triumph*. God has given us the Sprit of wisdom and revelation and we should shabach Him. There are times when we have to lift our voices and shout unto God with the voice of triumph.

Fidel Donaldson

Chapter 2
Praise Is My Platform

It is important to draw the distinction between the praise coming from the heart of a child of God and one that is coming from the heart of an individual who acknowledges God's existence, and thanks Him for doing something but isn't living a life committed and dedicated to Him. The child of God has a heart that is in a state of continual thankfulness for God's grace and mercy which is manifested in what He does for him; In *Psalm 34:1* David declared, *"I will bless the LORD at all times: his praise shall continually be in my mouth."* This is the praise posture that should be adopted by the child of God, one of blessing Him at all times and having His praise in our mouths continually. The child of God does not wait for God to do something specific but continually praise Him because he or she knows God is constantly working on her behalf. On the other hand, the sinner's thankfulness is kind of in the moment or a spur of the moment cursory acknowledgement of some blessing they are thankful for. The child of God recognizes that without God he or she can do nothing because it is in Him that we live, breathe and have our being.

For Glory and for Beauty

While praise can be expressed by anyone who is breathing and thankful in acknowledging that God has done something for them, worship can only be expressed by someone who is washed and redeemed by the Blood of Jesus, someone who knows God intimately through His Holy Spirit; the child of God uses praise as a platform to prepare to launch into worship. The unredeemed person does not have the Spirit of God, so that individual cannot enter into true Spirit worship because of flesh and carnality. They can praise God from the outer court but only the Blood washed redeemed can worship Him in the Holy of Holies, in the

Praise Worship and the Spirit of Prophecy

secret place in the beauty of holiness. Those that are sanctified and consecrated can enter His presence to worship Him and hear His prophetic voice. We see scriptural precedence for this when God instructed Moses to set aside Aaron and his sons to minister unto Him in the priest's office. Moses was instructed to make holy garments for them for glory and for beauty" *(Exodus 28:1-2).*

Worship takes us into His presence but we must be sanctified, consecrated and be covered in glory and beauty. The blood of Jesus Christ was shed to wash away our filthy sins, so through the power of the Holy Spirit we can be sanctified, purified, and beautified with glory for His presence. When the children of God assemble together for a service, getting into the presence of the Lord or having His presence manifest in the assembly, must be top priority; for that to take place, the congregants must be on one accord. Praise and worship should not begin when the worship leader and the praise team or choir is ready to commence. We should have praise and worship already going in our hearts so we will not have to be pumped and primed like a stopped up well to praise God. The Apostle Paul gave these instructions to the Church at Ephesus, *"And be not drunk with wine, wherein is excess; but be filled with the Spirit; Speaking to yourselves in psalms and hymns and spiritual songs, singing and making melody in your heart to the Lord"* *(Ephesians 5:18-19).* Here the Bible gives another example of the importance of the Spirit as it relates to worship. Once we are filled with the Spirit, our interaction with one another will not be based on carnal conversation that emanates from the flesh, but Godly conversation that emanates from the Spirit.

Paul gave similar instructions to the Colossians when he instructed them to, *"Let the word of Christ dwell in you richly in all wisdom; teaching and admonishing one another in psalms and hymns and spiritual songs, singing with grace in your hearts to the Lord" (Colossians 3:16).* Paul mentioned the word teaching when he wrote about psalms, hymns and spiritual songs and this gives further confirmation of the importance of receiving sound biblical teaching on the subject of Praise and Worship.

Fidel Donaldson

The Greek word for admonishing is *noutheteo* and it means *to put in mind, to caution or reprove gently, to warn*. The fact that Paul used a strong word like **admonishing** with the word *teaching* shows us how important it is for us to be taught.

There is further scriptural reference and support for the importance of believers ministering before the Lord and the creation of an atmosphere conducive to the moving of the Holy Spirit. Believers were first called Christians at Antioch, and there is a portion of scripture in the book of *Acts* which reinforces the aforementioned importance of believers ministering before the Lord, the moving of the Spirit, and the word of the Lord coming forth. In *Acts Chapter Thirteen* we are told of some prophets and teachers in the church that was at Antioch. The Bible declares, *"As they ministered to the Lord, and fasted, the Holy Ghost said, Separate me Barnabas and Saul for the work whereunto I have called them"* (Acts 13:2). The Greek word for Ministered as it is used there is *leitourgeo* and one of its meanings is to *worship*, or to be a *worshipper* of God. When the believers at Antioch worshipped and fasted, there was a moving of the Holy Spirit and a word of explicit instructions for the believers to separate Paul and Barnabas for the work they were called to perform. Jesus told His Disciples about certain spirits and the fact that it took fasting and prayer to cast them out. In the aforementioned reference we see worshiped coupled with fasting.

The Presence of the Lord

David is called the sweet psalmist of Israel and based on the plethora of psalms written by him, it is easy to deduce that he had a constant posture of praise and worship before the Lord. He made his share of mistakes, as we all do, but his love for and his commitment to the Lord is unquestioned. There are many scriptural examples of his dedication to the Lord and His desire to prepare a resting place for the Ark of God.

Praise Worship and the Spirit of Prophecy

"And David made him houses in the city of David, and prepared a place for the ark of God, and pitched for it a tent. Then David said None ought to carry the ark of God but the Levites: for them hath the LORD chosen to carry the ark of God, and to minister unto him for ever" (1 Chronicles 15:1-2). The ark contained the Shekinah, the Glorious presence of God and only sanctified Levites were chosen to carry it. The Levites carried the Ark on their shoulders but the Judah priesthood carries His presence inside of their temples. God's presence cannot be carried by the flesh. Carrying the Ark was not like carrying any other object. The carrying of the Ark was accompanied by a great religious celebration. The Judah priesthood is not made up of individuals who limit their praise to thanking God when He does something on their behalf; In the same manner in which the Yahweh chose the Jewish Levites to carry the Ark forever, Jesus the Lion of the tribe of Judah has chosen the Judah priesthood to carry the presence of the God-head and to minister to Him forever. What an awesome calling to have, to be chosen by God to carry His glorious presence forever.

"And David called for Zadok and Abiathar the priests, and for the Levites, for Uriel, Asaiah, and Joel, Shemaiah, and Eliel, and Amminadab, And said unto them, Ye are the chief of the fathers of the Levites: sanctify yourselves, both ye and your brethren, that ye may bring up the ark of the LORD God of Israel unto the place that I have prepared for it. For because ye did it not at the first, the LORD our God made a breach upon us, for that we sought him not after the due order. So the priests and the Levites sanctified themselves to bring up the ark of the LORD God of Israel. And the children of the Levites bare the ark of God upon their shoulders with the staves thereon, as Moses commanded according to the word of the LORD" (1 Chronicles 15:11-15). When David captured Jerusalem it became the political capital for the nation. Jerusalem means place of peace or foundation of peace. A tabernacle was erected on Mount Zion and the Ark would rest there, transforming Jerusalem into the

religious center of the nation. This was a precursor for what would take place in the future when Jesus Christ came to establish a new resting place for God's presence; the new resting place would be a remnant people called Zion; a people who have come to unity in the Spirit and the Ark of His presence would be at the center of their hearts. The aforementioned groups of people are the Judah priesthood chosen to carry His glorious presence.

The people God chooses to be a part of His priesthood must come before Him according to the instructions given to us in His holy word; failure to do so can cause a breach to come upon us. In preparation for the moving of the Ark, David called for the chief of the fathers of the Levites. The worship leader's position is vitally important because of his or her responsibility to set the atmosphere for what God desires to do in the midst of His people. If the atmosphere is not conducive to the entrance of the presence of the Lord, then what is the purpose of the meeting? The splendor of God's presence is weighty, so the shoulders of the Levites had to be strong enough carry it and the temple of the Judah priesthood must be strong enough to carry it. Judah should not be heavy laden with the cares of this world because that will hinder us from their responsibility of carrying God's glorious presence. Sanctification prepares us to bear the Ark by helping us to rid ourselves of the weight and sin that doth so easily beset us. The heaviest thing we should carry is the Shekinah Glory.

A Bump in the Road

When King David first attempted to bring the Ark of God to Jerusalem, he put it on a cart like the Philistines and that mode of transport ended in tragedy. I thank God for Grace and for mercy because I know there are times when we handle His presence like a Philistine, but instead of striking us he extends grace and mercy. Uzzah was struck when he tried to steady the Ark, as the oxen hit a bump in the road.

Praise Worship and the Spirit of Prophecy

A Good Thing Is not Always a God Thing

I am sure Uzzah thought he was doing a good thing when he touched the Ark in an attempt to steady it, but God had instructed Moses that no one outside of the Levites should touch the Ark; it is safe to say, since Uzzah was struck he was not a Levite. Obedience to God's command is of the utmost importance, and ignorance is not an excuse because we have the word of God to instruct us in the proper way to handle His presence. When we are not consecrated to carry the Ark and the Ark is being carried like a Philistine our procession will always hit a bump in the road and end in tragedy.

Search the Scriptures

Moses did not ask the Levites to transport the Ark; he gave them a command from God and once God gives a command there is no wiggle room; God's presence is not like Burger King where we can have it our way. Once David went and searched out the instructions given to Moses by God for the moving of the Ark, he prepared himself accordingly and the transportation of the Ark went well and the people were blessed. God's presence is an awesome place to be, but it can be a terrible place if we are operating outside of His will. He is no respecter of persons, and all of us, no matter our title or family connections, must sanctify ourselves before we come before His presence. Aaron's sons Nadab and Abihu learned this fact the hard way, *"And Nadab and Abihu, the sons of Aaron, took either of them his censer, and put fire therein, and put incense thereon, and offered strange fire before the LORD, which he commanded them not. And there went out fire from the LORD, and devoured them, and they died before the LORD"* (Leviticus 10:1-2). Obedience is better than sacrifice; Although Aaron was Moses' mouth piece and chosen to be the first High Priest, his sons were not exempted from following God's instructions on how He should be approached. Our God is a consuming fire, so everything that is not holy will be burned in that fire. The Holy Spirit convicts and reproves us of the things that are fleshly and carnal so can receive deliverance and not be hindered from entering God's presence to receive the fullness of Joy.

Ichabod: The Glory has Departed

God's children praise Him, so we can enter His presence to experience His riches in glory by Christ Jesus. One of Aaron's descendants by the name of Eli had two sons who had no respect for the presence of God and their actions caused the glory of God to depart from Israel. The Bible called them sons of Belial who knew not the LORD. It is hard to fathom how people could grow up in the house of the Lord with a father that is a high priest and not know God. Eli's sons Hophni and Phinehas had no regard for the things of God. In a battle with the Philistines they took the Ark on the battlefield like it was some lucky charm and the Philistine defeated them and took the Ark; Hophni and his brother Phinehas were killed on the battle field and when Phinehas' wife was in the delivery room about to give birth to a son, she received news that the Ark of God was taken and that her father in law and her husband were dead; she bowed her head and travailed and her labor pains became greater. When she was at the point of death the women at her side told her not to fear because she was delivering a son, but she was so heart-broken that she neither answered nor regarded them. She named the child Ichabod because the glory departed from Israel. Where there is no presence of God there is no glory and where there is no glory there is no quality of life. God is a holy God and his presence must be handled with reverence and the utmost respect.

Chapter 3
Worship God

Merriam Webster's online dictionary defines the word worship as *"reverence offered a divine being or supernatural power; also an act of expressing such reverence."* It comes from the old English word *weorthscipe.* Worship is the value or premium we place on God and our willingness to act accordingly. With that being said, there is more to true worship than what we feel and the songs we sing. True worship begins with a heart, body and soul that loves God and is dedicated to Him. A heart and mind that is being led by God's Holy Spirit, and a body that is subjected to that leading. I don't believe true worship can be expressed if the Holy Spirit's presence is not in our midst. He is the only one who can lead us before the throne of God's Divine Presence. Singing and dancing and feeling good is not an indication of true worship. The father seeks true worshipers. Those whose hearts are clean, washed by the blood of Jesus, and made sanctified by the Holy Spirit. He is seeking those who focus on the creator even though there might not be the beat and rhythm of a drum, the strum of a guitar, or the melodious tune of a fancy keyboard.

Paul told the church at Ephesus they were no longer strangers and foreigners, but fellow citizens with the saints, and of the household of God and that through Jesus Christ that household or building is fitly framed together and is growing unto a holy temple in the Lord. Believers who have received the promise of the Spirit through faith are being built together for a habitation of God through the Spirit. In times past the Most High God dwelt in temples made with hands and visited His people but Jesus came to make us a temple of habitation not one for visitation;

Fidel Donaldson

Jesus' blood was shed for our cleansing, but it is through the Spirit that we are being built into temples for His dwelling. We are to be holy temples offering worship to our Father in heaven.

I am always amazed how the Holy Spirit can give illumination on certain scriptures we have read over and over. I had this experience on a particular day as I was reading a portion of the Book of *Revelation*; prior to that day I always looked at the book of Revelation as a chronicling by John of a series of apocalyptic visions he received from God. I never thought the book of Revelation could give me revelation about worship and the Spirit and prophecy. On that particular day, I was reading *Chapter Nineteen* when my understanding became enlightened to the fact that there is a distinct connection between *worship, the Spirit of God* and the *prophetic*. The true prophetic voice is released through the Spirit and worship is a key facilitator.

I will go into more detail later about *Revelation 19*, but for now, allow me to set the stage. In *Revelation 19:10* there is recorded an incident where an angelic being is before John, and John fell at his feet to worship him. The angel tells John not to worship him because he is a fellow servant and one of his brethren that have the testimony of Jesus: Then he makes an emphatic statement to John, *"worship God: for the testimony of Jesus is the spirit of Prophecy."* The angel's instructions to John to "worship God" seems very obvious but when you see the level of idolatry in the world you realize how deceived many people are. Through unbelief, Satan the god of this world has blinded the minds of men, so they cannot see the glorious light of the gospel of Christ, who is the image of God.

God is the only one in the universe worthy of worship; angels should not be worshipped, Mary should not be worshipped! Idols, statues and certainly mankind should not be venerated through worship. Idolatry is the worship of any entity animate or inanimate outside of God. It is a dangerous practice and we readily see the danger of it when we read the

Praise Worship and the Spirit of Prophecy

Bible. Right in our modern churches, many are guilty of this when the leader of the church or the speaker of the hour is given a standing ovation or loud clapping as he or she approaches the rostrum or takes the podium. There is a time and place for this. The Bible tells us to honor those who labor amongst us, not worship them!

When the Israelites insisted that Aaron make them gods to go before them because they did not know what became of Moses *(Exodus 32:1KJV)*, Aaron made them a molten calf with an altar, and they corrupted themselves with revelry and immorality. When we make someone or something the object of worship and not God, corruption and immorality will follow. When Moses went up into the mount to meet with God, he was given specific instructions. God instructed him to tell the people they should have no other gods before Him; they should not make any graven images, or likeness of anything that is in heaven, on the earth or that is in the water under the earth. They should not bow down to them or serve them; *For I the LORD thy God am a jealous God, visiting the iniquity of the fathers upon the children unto the third and fourth generation of them that hate me" (Exodus 20:5)*. That is why Jehovah's witnesses go to great lengths to try to convince us that Jesus Christ is only a created being like the angels; that is why Muslims try to convince us Jesus was just a prophet, but the Apostle Paul told the Philippians, *"Wherefore God also hath highly exalted him, and given him a name which is above every name: That at the name of Jesus every knee should bow, of things in heaven, and things in earth, and things under the earth; and that every tongue should confess that Jesus Christ is Lord, to the glory of God the Father."* The pre-incarnate Christ was in the Godhead as the Word when God said, *"Let us make man in our image, after our likeness."* He was in the Godhead when the people tried to build a tower that reached heaven and the Godhead said, *"let us go down, and there confound their language, that they may not understand one another's speech."* When Jesus Christ ascended to heaven in glory, He went there not as the Word that was with God and is God but as Lord and Christ, worthy of all worship.

Fidel Donaldson

For every cause, there is an effect, and idolatry will not only affect us, but also those closest to us. It is apparent that God considers people who practice idolatry, as people who hate Him. Hate is a very strong word and it lets us know how serious a transgression it is to worship anyone or thing outside of Almighty God. Generations suffered because their forefathers practiced idolatry. When you search the scriptures, you never find anyone who practiced idolatry that did not have a terrible ending. Jezebel introduced the idolatrous practice of Baal worship to the nation of Israel. *"And of Jezebel also spake the LORD, saying, The dogs shall eat Jezebel by the wall of Jezreel"* (1 Kings 21:23). The prophetic word from God concerning the demise of Jezebel was fulfilled when Jehu instructed some eunuchs to throw her out of a window. When they went to bury her, the only things found were her skull, her feet and the palms of her hands, because dogs had eaten the rest of her.

In his letter to the church at Rome, Paul described what happened to people who practiced idolatry, and people who changed the glory of the uncorruptible God into an image made like unto corruptible man, to birds, fourfooted beasts, and creeping things. The Apostle said, *"Wherefore God also gave them up to uncleaness through the lusts of their own hearts, to dishonour their own bodies between themselves; this was done because they changed the truth of God into a lie, and worshipped and served the creature more than the Creator, who is blessed for ever. Amen (Romans 1:23-25).* When the Israelites cajoled Aaron into making gods to go before them, God was ready to destroy them and raise up a new nation until Moses interceded for them. When death and destruction were our wages for the sin of idolatry, God was going to wipe us out, but Jesus came and died for us.

There is an incident recorded in Acts Chapter 12 where Herod sat on his throne in royal apparel. When he spoke to the people, they shouted saying, *"it is the voice of a god, and not of a man."* The Bible

Praise Worship and the Spirit of Prophecy

declares, *"And immediately the angel of the Lord smote him, because he gave not God the glory: and he was eaten of worms, and gave up the ghost. But the word of God grew and multiplied."* When God gets the glory through worship, there will be growth and multiplication. Jezebel was eaten by dogs and Herod was eaten by worms! Worship puts the attention and focus on God and keeps us humble and broken before Him.

Worship gives Him the glory, and when received, our worship will facilitate the prophetic. When we stray from that path and put the attention on self and flesh, stagnation can occur and sometimes death if there is no true contrition and repentance.

If we are to be the type of worshippers who worship God in Spirit and in truth, we need to gain a Biblical understanding of true Spirit worship. I do not believe that it is left up to us to worship God in the manner we feel because feelings are fleeting and they can get us in a great deal of trouble. It is never about how we feel but all about who God is. He is the *Holy One of Israel*, the *Alpha* and the *Omega* and all worship belongs to Him. Feelings come from the soul which is man's *will*, his *intellect* and his *emotions*. Quite frankly, I can speak from a personal perspective that there are occasions that arise where worshipping God is far from my mind. Even though worship may not be on my mind, He is still worthy of my worship. I have to push past my feelings and worship Him in spite of my feelings.

Our emotions are governed by external factors so negative experiences and encounters can give us a feeling of melancholy where we just want to be left alone in our pity party. In those moments we do not feel like worshipping God; so if we go by feelings, God would only get worship when things are going well; this would put the focus and attention on us and not on God. I sincerely believe we have to be taught how to worship God; it is not something we gravitate to naturally, especially if our natures have not been delivered from the bondage of carnality. I used to think the book of Leviticus was just about sacrifices until I read somewhere that Leviticus is about worship. It gives a sinful people instructions on how they should approach a Holy God.

When God called Moses, Aaron and his sons, along with the seventy elders to come up to Him, He told them they should come and worship from afar; then he instructed them that Moses alone should come near to Him. Can you imagine if the others decided they would go up anyway? They would have been consumed by the fire of His presence like Aarons' sons-Nadab and Abihu! When the children of Israel came out of Egypt and went into the wilderness of Sinai, God told Moses He had chosen them to be a *peculiar treasure* unto Him above all people; they were to be a *kingdom of priests*, and an *holy nation*. One does not need to be peculiar, holy or priestly to **Praise** Him because the criteria for praise is breathing; to offer **Worship** in His presence one must be holy, a priest and be His peculiar treasure.

In preparation for His visiting the people, God said, *"And thou shalt set bounds unto the people round about, saying, Take heed to yourselves, that ye go not up into the mount, or touch the border of it: whosoever toucheth the mount shall be surely put to death"* (Exodus 19:1 KJV): God is holy and He dwells in unapproachable light, radiance and splendor. Jesus Christ came to remove the bounds which separate us from God, so we can dwell in His presence. Moses was told by God, *"When the trumpet soundeth long, they shall come up to the mount"* (Exodus 19:13). We are being prepared for the sound of the trumpet. *"For the Lord himself shall descend from heaven with a shout, with the voice of the archangel, and with the trump of God: and the dead in Christ shall rise first"* (1 Thessalonians 4:16). The Apostle John declared, *"After this I looked, and, behold, a door was opened in heaven: and the first voice which I heard was as it were of a trumpet talking with me; which said, Come up hither, and I will shew thee things which must be hereafter. And immediately I was in the spirit"* (Revelation 4:1).

Praise Worship and the Spirit of Prophecy

God is a Spirit, and His Kingdom is a spiritual realm and we must approach Him in worship through the Spirit. We don't approach God any way we feel like it; we approach Him according to the instructions given to us in the manual. Since the Bible is our instruction manual concerning all things related to God, we should endeavor to gain insight from the Bible on how God should be worshipped.

Let's go back to the Genesis or the beginning, where the word worship is first used in the Bible. *Genesis 22* tells the story of God instructing Abram to take his only son Isaac whom he loved into the land of Moriah; and offer him there for a burnt offering on one of the mountains. The word Moriah means chosen of God. God will choose the time and place in certain seasons of our lives to offer to Him the thing we hold most dear to our hearts. I can only imagine what went through Abram's mind when he received those instructions from God, after all, he and his wife Sarah had waited a long time to have a son, and now God was telling him to offer his only son as a burnt offering. God will test us with the things he blesses us with to determine if that thing has become the object of our worship.

In obedience to God, Abram took his beloved son Isaac and two of his young men and traveled to the place where God had instructed him to go. When he arrived there, he told the young men to: *"Abide ye here with the ass; and I and the lad will go yonder and worship, and come again to you"* (*Genesis 22:5*). He did not tell the young men that he was going to make a sacrifice, but to worship. The Hebrew word for worship as it is used there is *shachah* (pronounced shaw-khaw); and it means *to prostrate in homage to God, to bow, crouch or fall down, to reverence or make obeisance*. I've heard it said in some services that posture is not important, but I think it is important to note that the patriarch Abraham adopted a posture of prostration in the presence of God. I prefer to emulate the actions of a man like Abraham who is called a friend of God, than to listen to individuals speaking contrary to what I see and read in the scriptures.

Abram was ready and willing to give up the thing that was most precious, and he put it into the context of worship; this leads me to believe that true worship begins with a willingness to give God the thing that is most precious to us. I believe our most precious commodity in this world is the life God has given us because without it nothing else matters. With that in mind I believe worship at its very core is a life that is totally submitted to God. The outward physical posture and expression of worship like prostrating, crouching or bowing down must flow from a heart and mind that love God and are willing to yield to His will His purpose and His plan, no matter how difficult they may seem or when they are not readily understood by the natural mind. The natural mind cannot fathom why God would give a son then require him to be sacrificed. The renewed mind understands that everything belongs to God.

Without obedience, sacrifice is meaningless. A worshipper who is committed to God will trust Him as Abram did when the request challenges every fiber of their being; Worshippers do not value or esteem people or earthly possessions above our Heavenly Father. People who only praise God for what He has done will turn their backs to Him when He does not do or give them something they truly desire. Job did not heed his wife's advice when she asked him why he did not curse God and die because he was a worshipper of God. I remember watching several interviews after the September 11 attack on the World Trade Center, and some of the people being interviewed sounded like they could no longer put their trust in God because of the immensity of their lost. Job lost everything and everyone he had but his wife, and she was not much of a comfort to him as he sat in an ash heap scraping the puss laden sores on his body with a potsherd. Instead of cursing God like his wife suggested, he decided to bless the name of the LORD; as previously stated, Job was a true worshipper. In prosperous times we can all worship God, but when

Praise Worship and the Spirit of Prophecy

tragedy strikes, can we say: *"Naked came I out of my mother's womb, and naked shall I return thither: the LORD gave, and the LORD hath taken away; blessed be the name of the LORD" (Job 1:21)*. There is a temptation to charge God foolishly when tragedy strikes, but we must endeavor to show our trust through a continual posture of worship. The loss of a loved one whether a son, daughter, husband wife can cause our faith to be shaken but worshippers will not allow the tragic nature of any situation to cause them to turn from God; on the contrary, they will turn to God. Job asked the question, *"Shall not the Judge of all the earth do right?"* the answer is a resounding, "Yes!" We will not always be able to understand why some things befall us and our loved ones but worshippers know we must trust God where we cannot trace Him. We must trust Him because He is the righteous Judge and He allows some things to take place by His will that He could have prevented by His power. With that said, I also believe that worship is faith and trust in the sovereignty of God and His ability to make all things beautiful in their season. This is true worship!!!

The Worship Leader

The position of worship leader is one of the most important in the church because he or she is responsible for setting an atmosphere through praise and worship that will facilitate the entrance of the presence of the Lord into our sphere. Worship leaders are not called to entertain us or have the spotlight on them. We must be careful not to get to a place where we begin to idolize the person leading worship because of their charisma and music ability. The worship leader's job is to set the atmosphere in worship so the presence of God can permeate and saturate the meeting place; this prepares the people to receive a prophetic word, a word of wisdom or a word of knowledge from the Lord. When it gets to the place where it is about the congregants and the person leading the worship, then we may as well be at a concert, because the soul is being entertained and God is not getting the glory through worship, the Spirit is not moving and there is no prophetic voice.

Fidel Donaldson

Words of Wisdom from a Mother to her Son

Recently I had an opportunity to speak with my friend and fellow minister prophetess Robin Perry, and she told me of a conversation she had with her son concerning true Spirit led worship. Prophetess Robin said, "I explained and reiterated the Word to him about God seeking true worshippers! I told Rhakeem that he should never get caught up with the congregation cheering him on because then his focus would be singing to glorify them: which is only entertainment and performing, but when he sings he should minister to God, and the Spirit of God will move through him, and the atmosphere will shift! I explained to him that true and pure worship to God will always permeate any atmosphere; and God shall get ALL the glory! I told him my desire is to live a righteous life and to leave a legacy, not just to make a living! That came forth because we also discussed how some ministers of music today only play for pay! I was not negating the fact that they were worthy to be compensated some way, but was stressing to him to never play and sing just for a check!"

Praise Worship and the Spirit of Prophecy

PART TWO

Fidel Donaldson

Chapter 4

A Voice Like A Trumpet

Worship is more about who we are than it is about what we do. As children of God our lives must be set apart for His plan and purpose; worship should come from a heart of love for God because when we truly love God we don't find it difficult to be transparent in His presence, and we will not be afraid of expressing that love.

The Apostle John is described as the disciple whom Jesus loved, and I know that He loved His Lord. During meetings, John would lean on the bosom of His Lord as a sign of love and adoration. When we love Jesus and are willing to serve Him, He will reveal things to us and through us by the Spirit. In the book of Revelation we get an understanding of the correlation between worship, the Spirit, and the prophetic voice.

John was on an island called Patmos when he received a revelation of Jesus pertaining to things that would come to pass in the future. This revelation was given to John so that he could show it to the servants. Worshippers must have a servant's heart in-order to receive true revelation. When Jesus turned the water into wine at the marriage feast, the governor did not know what was done, but the servants knew. When Naaman was wroth and went away because Elisha told him to wash in Jordan seven times, it was his servants who came near to him and convinced him to go back and get his healing. In *Revelation Chapter 1* John is described as a servant.

John was not on vacation on the isle of Patmos, he was banished there as a prisoner because of the word of God and the testimony of Jesus Christ. Bona fide prophets may have to spend time in the wilderness like Moses and John the Baptist, in captivity like Ezekiel and Daniel, and on an island in a cave like the Apostle John. Although John's environment and his surroundings were very tough, he was able to say, *"I was in the Spirit on the Lord's day, and heard behind me a great voice, as of a trumpet"* (*Revelation 1:10*). John's statement confirms the connection between being in the Spirit and the hearing of a sound or a word from heaven. When the Spirit of the Lord comes upon us, there should be a sound or a word that manifest. When the Spirit of the LORD came upon Gideon, he blew a trumpet; David's last words in the Bible began with this statement, *"The Spirit of the LORD spake by me, and his word was in my tongue"* (*2 Samuel 23:2*). What an awesome confirmation of the word of the Lord coming forth through His Spirit! According to the book of Genesis, when the earth was without form and void and darkness was upon the face of the deep, the Spirit of God moved upon the waters and God said, *"Let there be light."* When Jesus was baptized by John, the heavens were opened unto Him, and he saw the Spirit of God descending on Him like a dove and a voice from heaven spoke. When the Spirit of the Lord came upon the disciples assembled in the upper room, they heard a sound from heaven as of a mighty rushing wind. The Spirit and the Word work together in unity and agreement.

Praise Worship and the Spirit of Prophecy

No matter how rough or difficult our situation, if we can get in the Spirit, we can hear a sound or a word from heaven. Worship is the key to gain us entrance into that place. When we take our eyes off our current trials and struggles and worship God, the Spirit will move and He will speak prophetically to us and through us. It is important that we understand and embrace this connection because in this day and hour disciples will find themselves dealing with great trials and tribulations, but must endeavor to stay in the Spirit through a heart of worship. The Spirit can translate us from one place to another as was done for the Prophet Ezekiel. When we allow ourselves to be heavy laden by problems, it becomes difficult for us to move in the Spirit and receive the word being spoken by God.

Like John, the Prophet Ezekiel was able through the Spirit to rise above a place of captivity and receive something from heaven. Ezekiel was among a group of captives but did not adopt their posture and their melancholy mindset. *Psalm 137* gives us a picture of the captive's posture and their state of mind; instead of worshipping God they said, *"By the rivers of Babylon, there we sat, yea, we wept, when we remembered Zion. We hanged our harps upon the willows in the midst thereof. For there they that carried us away captive required of us a song; and they that wasted us required of us mirth, saying, Sing us one of the songs of Zion. How shall we sing the Lord's song in a strange land?*

Fidel Donaldson

It is easy to sing the LORD'S song in a place that is nice and comfortable, but can you sing it in a strange land like a prison where you have been separated from loved ones for a very long time; can you sing it from a body that is held captive by some crippling disease, sickness or infirmity? From emotions trapped in a prison of sadness due to abandonment or the death of a loved one? Do not allow your environment or your condition to cause you to hang your praise and worship on a willow tree. Find a place in worship and like Ezekiel you will be taken up in the Spirit and see visions; encourage yourself in the Lord like David or hear a great voice of a trumpet like John.

When a great voice is speaking from heaven, we must pay attention. Christians believe that heaven is our home and the Bible is the book that tells us what it is like and what we need to do to get there. Since we are being prepared by the Holy Spirit to live in the presence of God, we need to know what is taking place in His presence and the revelation given to John gives us a great snapshot. Since the thesis of this book is worship and the prophetic voice in us, I am focusing my attention on the encounter John had with an angelic being while on the Isle of Patmos, as recorded in *Revelation 19*.

One Sound

John said he heard a great voice of much people in heaven, saying, *Alleluia; salvation, and glory, and honour, and power, unto the Lord our God (Revelation 19:1)*. John did not say he heard the voice of angels, but the voice of much people. These are the people who have overcome by the blood of the Lamb and the word of their testimony and loved not their life unto death. These people are not spectators, they are not meditating, but they are participating in the chorus of praise and worship to the Lamb seated on the throne.

I was intrigued by the fact that, although there are a large number of people speaking, John does not use the plural voices, but the singular word voice. The redeemed people in heaven who are worshipping the Lamb that is seated on the throne are in such a state of unity and oneness that John hears them as a single great voice. It is important that our sound be the sound of unity if we expect to hear from heaven. At the dedication of the temple of Solomon they received the glorious results that come from making one sound, *"It came even to pass, as the trumpeters and singers were as one, to make one sound to be heard in praising and thanking the LORD; and when they lifted up their voice with the trumpets and cymbals and instruments of musick, and praised the LORD, saying, For he is good; for his mercy endureth for ever: that then the house was filled with a cloud, even the house of the LORD; So that the priests could not stand to minister by reason of the cloud: for the glory of the LORD had filled the house"* (2 Chronicles 5:13-14). Unity and oneness in worship will cause a cloud of glory to fill our temple so our goal in corporate worship must be to get on one accord in unity so we can be in tune with the great voice and trumpet like sound that is emanating from heaven.

Fidel Donaldson

When John heard the great voice like a trumpet, the focus was not on the people singing but on the Almighty God. This is the pattern for us to imitate. Our worship must be vertical and not horizontal. All the glory and the honor must go to God and not flesh. Worship belongs to our God.

The Fall of Babylon

Revelation 19 starts with the words, *"And after these things I heard."* I needed to know what events transpired before John heard the voice of the heavenly choir so I checked out *Revelation 18* and saw that it dealt with the fall of Babylon. Babylon represented an evil world's system and everything associated with it. John saw the fall of this evil corrupt system and after the fall he was tuned in to the great voice coming from heaven. Believers must be careful not to be ensnared by the modern day Babylonian system which has infected all strata of society. Show business, politics and the economic sector is driven by self, economic greed and a lust for power. Now we have rap stars who have become business moguls blaspheming the name of Jesus Yeshua and calling themselves god in the flesh. We have Hollywood films and political pundits that cast aspersions on Christians because we refuse to compromise on the hot button issues of the day. Let God be true and every man be a liar. These systems will crumble one day, and only the true worshippers of God will stand.

The great voice that John heard not only gave glory to God, but declared this concerning Him, *"For true and righteous are his judgments: for he hath judged the great whore, which did corrupt the*

Praise Worship and the Spirit of Prophecy

earth with her fornication, and hath avenged the blood of his servants at her hand" (Revelation 19:2).

You don't have to look far today to witness the corruption that is in the earth. Men love sinful pleasures more than they love God, and when His servants take a stand for Him they are persecuted and even killed. The voice John heard in heaven was getting greater and greater. At first it was a great voice of much people, by the time we get to *verse 6,* it is the voice of many waters, and as the voice of mighty thunderings.

Some people get offended if the praise and worship is considered too loud. In some denominations they don't use instruments and the people are not at liberty to praise and worship God; everything is cool and controlled; you may as well have gone to a library or a university lecture. Revelation gives us a snapshot of what heaven sounds like. This is to all of the people who try to stifle praise and worship when they deem it to be too loud and radical. Read *Revelation 19* and you will soon discover that everyone in heaven is lifting their voice to make one sound in praising God. Heaven is not a quiet place; it is not a place where people do their own thing; it is a place of loud praise and worship of the Lamb that is seated on the throne. Can you imagine hearing a voice of many waters or a voice like a mighty thundering? I know how frightening it can be when there is a sudden burst of thunder that catches us off guard. Have you ever been to the beach and heard the mighty sound of the waves crashing into the shoreline?

With that in mind, I can only imagine what it is like to actually hear the sound being made in heaven before the throne.

Shout it Out

When I was much younger there was a commercial on TV with a slogan that said, *"If you want a tough stain out shout it out."* The commercial was for a laundry detergent named *"Shout."* The disciple's shout is a powerful weapon that can be used against our adversary if we understand the revelation of the shout. As children, most of us were taught to speak softly and that it was undignified to shout, but there is a proper time and place for a good shout and the Bible confirms this. God called David, *"a man after mine own heart."* David was called that because he had a desire to fulfill God's will and because he had a heart with a voracious appetite for the praise and worship of God. When he instructs us in *Psalm 47:1* to shout unto God with the voice of triumph he used the Hebrew word *ruah* and it means *blow an alarm*, (*cry aloud, out*), destroy, *make a joyful noise, shout for joy, to mar* (*especially by breaking*).

Triumph begins in the mind and not with the way we feel; and the shout of triumph can break down walls and strongholds. Years ago there was a commercial by a company called Memorex. The commercial was for a cassette tape and there was a slogan titled, *"is it live or is it Memorex?"* A glass was placed on a table and the voice of the great singer Ella Fitzgerald was heard singing and when a certain note was reached, the glass shattered; keep in mind it was a shout that brought down the wall of Jericho. The shout of triumphant praise and worship will cause things that are working against us to be shattered. If you have walls or barriers you need to come down or a tough situation you need to get out of, open your mouth, lift your voice like a trumpet and shout it out.

Shachah and Proskuneo

When John heard the second wave of the great voice, the voice of thunderings and many waters; the content of their speech did not change, they continued to shout *Alleluia*; they continued to give God the highest praise. As the worship was taking place, the four and twenty elders and the four beasts fell down and worshipped God that sat on the throne, saying *Amen*; *Alleluia*. What an awesome confirmation of the *Shachah* of the Old Testament and the *Proskuneo* of the New Testament! When the four and twenty elders and the four beasts fell down and worshipped God, a voice came out of the throne saying, *"Praise our God, all ye his servants, and ye that fear him, both great and small" (Revelation 19:5).* Note the use of the word servants and the fact that as the worship builds to a crescendo, the focus stays on God. Worship brought a voice from the throne in heaven and when we adopt that posture, the posture of worshipping God in the unity of the Spirit, we will receive a voice from the throne in heaven. We may not have the crowns like the elders, but if people like the elders, who have reached the pinnacle which is a place before the throne of God, can fall prostrate in worship, then why can't we?

Fidel Donaldson

Does the event in heaven described by John reflect a picture of what we see in our services? Does it reflect a picture of us personally in our time of devotion? Do you see people in a posture of *Shachah* and *Proskuneo* or dancing before the Lord our God? I know there are congregations where this type of worship takes place but it should be the rule and not the exception. Since heaven is our goal and in heaven crowns are being cast down and elders are falling down and worshipping God, then shouldn't we be free in our services to express our love and adoration for God in the local assembly as the redeemed people are expressing themselves in heaven?

The Marriage Supper of the Lamb

Besides describing the fact that Babylon is judged and the blood of the saints has been avenged. The heavenly chorus was rejoicing because the marriage of the lamb was come and the bride made herself ready. As the redeemed of the Lord we are being prepared to be a part of the Bride of Christ at the marriage supper and this is why we must endeavor to walk in holiness and righteousness. With the help of the Holy Spirit, we have to make ourselves ready. One day soon, the filthy garment of the flesh will give way to the fine clean white linen which will be the righteousness of the saints.

In the midst of such a great praise and worship celebration, it is no wonder John was ready to fall down and worship the angelic being that was before Him. The angel let him know that only God is to be worshipped. Not only did he tell John to, *"Worship God,"* but he also told him, *"The testimony of Jesus is the spirit of prophecy."* Blood

Praise Worship and the Spirit of Prophecy

washed believers have their testimony of Jesus and the Spirit of God is dwelling on the inside of them and with Him comes the spirit of prophecy. Prophecy comes from the Spirit and worship moves the Spirit and stirs the prophetic voice on the inside.

When David was bringing the ark of God to Jerusalem, it was a procession of joy with dancing, singing, shouting and the playing of musical instruments. The Bible declares, *"Thus all Israel brought up the ark of the covenant of the LORD with shouting, and with sound of the cornet, and with trumpets, and with cymbals, making a noise with psalteries and harps. And it came to pass, as the ark of the covenant of the LORD came to the city of David, that Michal the daughter of Saul looking out at a window saw king David dancing and playing: and she despised him in her heart"* (1 Chronicles 15:28-29). Instead of being out with the procession of praise and worship, she chose to peep out a window with disdain and disgust in her heart. When David came home, she accused him of disrobing himself before the maidens like a vain and shameless person. I guess she figured as a king he should have left the free expression of praise and worship to others; listen to David's response to her, *"It was before the LORD, which chose me before thy father, and before all his house, to appoint me ruler over the people of the LORD, over Israel: therefore will I play before the LORD. And I will be yet more vile than thus, and will be base in mine own sight: and of the maidservants which thou hast spoken of, of them shall I be had in honour"* (2 Samuel 6:21-22).

Fidel Donaldson

It is important to note that the last thing that is said in that chapter is this, *"Therefore Michal the daughter of Saul had no child unto the day of her death."* I truly believe worship will cause us to be fruitful through the prophetic and I also believe that a heart full of anger, hatred and jealousy can cause us to be barren.

Chapter 5
Spirit and Truth Worship

We connect and interact with other human beings on a physical level, but God is a Spirit, and though we utilize physical gestures in our communication with Him and in our adoration of Him, those physical gestures must have Spirit translation to be meaningful to God, for example, we use words when we pray, but Paul declared, *"Likewise the Spirit also helpeth our infirmities: for we know not what we should pray for as we ought: but the Spirit itself maketh intercession for us with groanings which cannot be uttered. And he that searcheth the hearts knoweth what is the mind of the Spirit, because he maketh intercession for the saints according to the will of God"*(Romans 8:26-27).

Although we use words as a mode of communication in prayer, the Holy Spirit helps us by being the intermediary in-order to make those prayers effective. I believe He helps our infirmities in worship in the same manner. I don't believe praise and worship comes natural to most people because the flesh is always warring against the spirit and Satan hates the fact God is being worshipped. Remember he once held a very prestigious position in heaven as the Son of the morning, the anointed Cherub that had all manner of stringed instruments in him. He was cast down from that lofty place because pride was found in Him when he attempted to exalt himself above the throne of God. When God is not on the throne of someone's heart, pride will rule. Pride is one of the chief enemies of praise and worship. It is not hard to understand why the adversary fights so hard to pervert music and to hinder praise and worship. Because of the importance of Spirit led praise and worship and what it means to us individually and corporately, we need anointed individuals to teach us the dynamics of Spirit led praise and worship. These individuals must be humble and flow in a spirit of meekness and humility; because if they do not, when the accolades come they will attempt to take the glory for themselves.

The Holy Spirit

Since the Holy Spirit plays such an integral part prophetically, and in every other facet of the believer's life, it is important that I give the reader a brief synopsis of His ministry; I would like to stress the word brief. The Holy Spirit's ministry in the lives of believers individually and corporately should not be taken for granted. There are many occasions where I've heard believers refer to the Holy Spirit as "it" or some believers will say, *"Something told me."* The Holy Spirit is the Third Person in the God-head and third does not mean He is somehow less in essence than God our Father and our Lord Jesus Christ. While the Holy Spirit's function is distinct and unique from that of the Father and the Lord Jesus, He is of the same essence as the Father and the Lord Jesus. When Jesus ascended to heaven in glory, the ministry of the Holy Spirit came to the forefront to prepare believers through a process of sanctification to be a part of the universal church being built by the Lord. In his book, *The Foundations of Christian Doctrine* published by Bible Temple Publishing, author Kevin J. Conner has this to say about the Holy Spirit, *"The Holy Spirit is the third divine person of the eternal Godhead, co-equal, and co-existent with the Father and the Son. It is His ministry to convict and convert man as well as to reveal the Son and the Father to the believer. Since the glorification of the Lord Jesus Christ, the Holy Spirit in all His glorious operations is working through all who believe on the Father through the Son. This is why the present era is known as the age of the Holy Spirit."*

Since the children of God are living in the age of the Holy Spirit, it is incumbent upon us to both learn of Him and to yield to His leading.

The Spirit of Revelation

One of the multi-faceted characteristics of the Holy Spirit is that "He is the Spirit of Revelation." In his first letter to the church at Corinth, the apostle Paul informed them of the hidden wisdom of God which was ordained before the world unto our glory. The Corinthians were told that Paul and his companions spoke or revealed the hidden wisdom of God in a mystery. It was hidden from the princes of this world, so they would not hinder Jesus from being crucified. According to Paul, *"God hath revealed them unto us by His Spirit: for the Spirit searcheth all things, yea, the deep things of God" (1 Corinthians 2:10).* The wisdom of God is unsearchable, hence it cannot be discerned by the natural mind, but the children of God in whom the Spirit of God dwells they can discern the deep things of God through the Spirit. Paul went on to inform them that the children of God have not received the spirit of the world but the Spirit of God which allows them to know the things God has freely given to them. The natural man can have more degrees than a thermometer, and he may have a very high IQ, but he does not receive the things of the Spirit according to Paul because they are foolishness to him; he cannot know them because they can only be discerned through the Spirit. Discernment of the Spirit should be one of the gifts manifesting in the lives of God's children. The Spirit allows the child of God to tap into the deep things of God and bring them forth prophetically and in any other manner orchestrated by the Holy Spirit. We miss out on a great deal when we limit the Spirit in our lives, because we desire to do things through our human will intellect or through our emotions.

The Holy Spirit's manifestation in the lives of disciples should not be reduced solely to speaking in tongues. Speaking in tongues is a precious gift, but the Holy Spirit has a great deal more for us in terms of manifestation. Prophetic utterance, words of wisdom and knowledge are other manifestations and we should experience. Imagine if someone gave you a very valuable gift and you only utilized a small portion of it while the rest remained unused. A diligent search of the scriptures will reveal the many aspects of the Holy Spirit. The Bible calls Him the *Comforter*, He is a *Teacher*, He is the *Spirit of truth*, and He is a *Guide*; Prophetess Dwann Rollinson of The Worship Place Church in Jacksonville, Florida calls the Holy Spirit, *"the Divine Director."* I love that terminology because the Bible declares, *"the steps of a good man are ordered by the LORD: and he delighteth in His way"* (Psalm 37:23). How does God order the steps of His people? I truly believe He does it through His Holy Spirit who is living on the inside of the children of God. Walking in the path God has prepared for us is dependent on our ability to receive the instructions of the Holy Spirit and a willingness to obey. How can we obey His voice if we do not spend time speaking with Him? In order for us to delight ourselves in God's way we must discern His way, and the Holy Spirit is the one who gives us the discernment. Whether prophecy, prayer, worship or any other activity undertaken in the name of Jesus, the Holy Spirit must be our Divine Director.

Personal Testimony

Recently I was on the 5a.m. prayer line and the Holy Spirit spoke through me about the story recorded in the Bible in *Acts Chapter 12* when Herod killed James and imprisoned Peter. The saints responded by praying without ceasing, and convening a prayer meeting in the home of Mary the mother of John. God heard their prayers and sent an angel to deliver Peter. When he arrived at the door of the prayer meeting he had to keep knocking because they would not open the door. By the unction of the Holy Spirit I told the disciples on the prayer line that in this season God would send the answer to the door and we must be able to discern and open the door and receive. When I got off the prayer line that morning, I received a call from a minister and friend who informed me she was in her prayer closet and the Lord spoke to her and she had to obey God. Thirty minutes later she was at my door ringing the bell. When I opened the door she stepped in, handed me an envelope and told me the Lord spoke to her in her prayer closet and instructed her to bless me with six hundred dollars. We were in a deep place of worship that morning and the word of the Lord came out of that place of deep worship.

Spirit and Truth

Although Jesus walked in great authority and power in the earth He was the meekest and humblest person who ever walked the earth.

Fidel Donaldson

Lucifer said, *"I will"* but Jesus said, *"Not my will."*

When Jesus ministered to the woman of Samaria, He corrected her lack of understanding of true worship. She saw Jesus as a prophet and attempted to tell Him about a particular place of worship. She was partially correct in her assessment of Him because He had the Spirit without measure so He was the true Master Prophet. Jesus told her, "*Woman, believe me, the hour cometh, when ye shall neither in this mountain, nor yet at Jerusalem, worship the Father. Ye worship ye know not what: we know what we worship: for salvation is of the Jews. But the hour cometh, and now is, when the true worshippers shall worship the Father in spirit and in truth: for the Father seeketh such to worship him. God is a Spirit: and they that worship him must worship him in spirit and in truth*" (John 4:21-24). PC Study Bible V5 says this concerning true worship, "With the advent of the Messiah the time came for a new order of worship. True worshippers are those who realize that Jesus is the Truth of God and the one and only way to the Father. To worship in Truth is to worship God through Jesus. To worship in Spirit is to worship in the new realm which God has revealed to people. God is Spirit is a better translation than the KJV's "God is a Spirit." God is not one Spirit among many. Worship of God can be done only through Jesus who expresses God's invisible nature and by virtue of the Holy Spirit who opens to a believer the new realm of the kingdom."

According to Jesus, true worship has to come from the Spirit, and an individual who does not have God's Spirit will not be able to offer up true worship to Him because the spirit of an unredeemed person can praise God for what He has done, but cannot commune with God and

Praise Worship and the Spirit of Prophecy

worship Him for who He is. To worship Him, we must know Him intimately in the beauty of holiness. If we desire to get into the presence of God and receive the fullness of joy that comes from such an encounter we must endeavor to become what God is seeking. God is not seeking individuals of wealth and prestige, or individuals who are pillars in society, but He is seeking true worshippers. It is important to reiterate that worship is not external but begins internally with a heart and mind that is yielded to God.

The fact that God is seeking true worshippers lets me know that any individual, irrespective of class, color or creed, can be received by God if they are willing to worship Him in spirit and in truth. In some societies if you are not a part of a certain caste then you cannot move up the social strata. In other societies it is difficult to attain upward mobility without higher education or being connected to people of influence. God does not use any of the aforementioned criteria for the people He is seeking; His criterion is spirit and truth worship which emanates from a heart oflove and adoration. Spirit and truth worship propels the worshipper into the presence of the Lord.

Prior to her encounter with Jesus at the well, the woman of Samaria was stuck in an archaic religious paradigm of ignorance concerning what God was seeking. After her encounter with Jesus, she was liberated from the bondage of religious ignorance which radically transformed her life.

John used the Greek word *proskuneo* for worship and it means *to kiss like a dog licking his master's hand: to fawn or crouch: to prostrate oneself in homage or to do reverence.* It has the same connotation as the Hebrew word shachah used by Abraham and recorded in *Genesis 22:15.*

When self is on the throne, one can still praise God for what He has done, but only a person willing to die to self so they can live through the Spirit will be humble enough to shachah or proskuneo God. Pride will hinder someone from bowing in worship to kiss the feet of Jesus.

During the high praise and worship of any service or gathering, you can readily see the difference between bystanders, praisers, and true worshippers. True worshippers are not intimidated or concerned about the way they look to others. They have a Spirit led desire to get in the presence of the Lord and they refuse to be denied. They have a heightened sensitivity to the Spirit which is evidenced by their desire to prostrate themselves, often weeping with tears of joy and appreciation.

Bystanders adopt a posture of stoicism with a look of discomfort, refusing to clap their hands and move their feet as the rhythm of the praise and worship permeates and saturates the atmosphere. Lovers of praise and worship respond to the music as it hits their heart and soul, but the worshippers do not stay at that place; as they begin to sense the goodness of God in the praise and worship they move into the Holy of Holies to be in a place of intimacy with His Divine

Presence. They come broken with a heart of contrition and repentance.

Praise Worship and the Spirit of Prophecy

We see a beautiful illustration of this recorded in *Luke Chapter 7 beginning at verse 36.* Jesus is invited to dinner by a Pharisee. It was the custom of the day when one had a dinner party, to provide for the guests' feet to be cleaned before the meal because most people wore sandals and the roads were unpaved. The Pharisee did not arrange for Jesus' feet to be cleaned. Pharisees had great knowledge of the scriptures and adhered to a strict interpretation of the laws given by God to Moses and added their own ordinances to it; this caused many of them to be puffed up with religious pride.

Let the Oil Flow

A woman arrived at the dinner uninvited after she learned that Jesus was eating there. She was not a woman of stature, wealth or prestige because the Pharisee characterized her as a sinner. Her actions are proof to me that she may have been a sinner before she came to that house, but when she found out that Jesus was there she came in a spirit of meekness and repentance. She stood behind Jesus with a jar of very expensive oil of perfume, and as she stood behind Him her tears began to fall, signifying to me that she had a heart of contrition, and once you have that type of heart you can worship Him. The oil of perfume was very expensive so it was a sacrifice for the man. She was willing to give Jesus something very precious and expensive which revealed a true heart of worship.

Pouring oil or perfume on someone's head was a normal sign of respect, but this woman did not only come to show respect to Jesus,but she came to worship Him. How did she express worship?

Fidel Donaldson

She anointed His feet with the oil, crouched down and wiped her tears off His feet with her hair and constantly kissed His feet; as a sign of love, submission and affection. The religious Pharisee did none of these things for Jesus but the woman understood what true worship meant!

Search the scriptures and you will see several instances where individuals came to Jesus and fell down and worshipped Him; It first happened when He was a baby and received a visit from some wise men. In describing the actions of the wise men who came from the East to see baby Jesus, John declared, "*And when they were come into the house, they saw the young child with Mary his mother, and fell down, and worshipped Him: and when they opened their treasures, they presented unto Him gifts; gold, and frankincense, and myrrh*" (*Matthew 2:11*).

Wise men with Godly wisdom will worship Jesus and bestow their treasures upon Him because through the Spirit they can discern who He is and what He means to their lives and the lives of others. Worship is not only physical act, but it is a willingness to live a life that is dedicated and committed to Him and to open our treasures and bless Him. The wise men needed a star to lead them to Jesus, but thank God we have the Holy Spirit to lead us into His presence. He is our comforter and our guide into all things concerning Jesus. Through the Spirit's leading we can receive the prophetic word from the mouth of God.

Praise Worship and the Spirit of Prophecy

Ezekiel and Jeremiah were two prophets commanded by the LORD to speak prophetically and when God gives a command it's bestto obey Him. As we mature in the things of the Spirit, we will be able to discern when it is God and when it is our emotion, our will or our intellect. When the Spirit of the Lord speaks, He is never wrong; we may miss the mark at times, but He always hits the prophetic bulls-eye. The key to prophetic accuracy is making sure we are speaking under His unction and not of our own soul. True prophets can miss the mark sometimes. When the LORD sent the prophet Samuel to Jessie's house to anoint the new king, Samuel saw Eliab and said, *"Surely the LORD's anointed is before him. But the LORD said unto Samuel, Look not on his countenance, or on the height of his stature; because I have refused him: for the LORD seeth not as man seeth; for man looketh on the outward appearance, but the LORD looketh on the heart" (1 Samuel 16:6-7).* The natural eye will be enamored with the countenance of an individual but the spirit of prophecy allows us to see beyond the façade to discern what is in the heart.

Rivers of Living Water

I often tell people that God has not empowered us with the gift of the Holy Ghost only to do for us what He has empowered us to do for ourselves. One of the characteristics of the Holy Ghost is boldness to speak the word. A person can have a personality that is introverted,

but when the Holy Ghost comes upon her, she will speak the word with boldness if she does not quench the Spirit out of fear. Listen to what Jesus said concerning the receiving of the Holy Spirit, *"In the last day, that great day of the feast, Jesus stood and cried, saying, If any man thirst, let him come unto me, and drink. He that believeth on me, as the scripture hath said, out of his belly shall flow rivers of living water. (But this spake he of the Spirit, which they that believe on him should receive: for the Holy Ghost was not yet given; because that Jesus was not yet glorified.) Many of the people therefore, when they heard this saying, said, Of a truth this is the Prophet"* (John 7:37-40).

Jesus was revealing to the assembly exactly what He revealed to the woman of Samaria at the well, He is the only one who can give us living water through the Holy Spirit. When Jesus spoke under the unction of the Holy Spirit, the people identified Him as the Prophet, not a prophet but the Prophet Moses spoke about when he told the people, *"The LORD thy God will raise up unto thee a Prophet from the midst of thee, of thy brethren, like unto me; unto him ye shall hearken"* *(Deuteronomy. 18:15).* Some of the people saw Him as the Prophet, but did not yield to Him as Savior. It is interesting to note that the woman at the well and the people at the feast recognized the prophetic anointing when Jesus spoke. When we speak under the unction of the Holy Spirit, discerning people will recognize the prophetic anointing.

Jesus rose from the grave and is seated at the right hand of God in a glorified body, and the Holy Spirit is the gift He has given to His people so the rivers of living water can flow out of our belly. Let the river flow!!!

Praise Worship and the Spirit of Prophecy

Chapter 6

The Spirit of Prophecy

Prophecy is a gift from God and we should not shy away from it because of a lack of understanding concerning the true prophetic, or because of negative experiences we have had with the spirit of false prophecy. Wherever there is something genuine, something counterfeit will not be far away. False prophecy should not cause us to miss out on this wonderful gift of prophecy given to the Church by the Lord Jesus Christ.

My sincere desire is to bring some clarity to this gift from God and to show through Biblical exposition and exegesis why it is for the body of Christ today, not just for a few chosen individuals during Old Testament Times. Our understanding of the prophetic must begin with a Biblical definition of the word prophecy.

Old and New Testament Words for Prophecy

1) In *2 Chronicles 9:29* the Hebrew word *nebuw'ah* is used for prophecy (pronounced *neb-oo-aw'*); It means *a prediction spoken or written*. It comes from the root word *naba* (pronounced *naw-baw'*); It means *to speak or sing by inspiration in prediction or simple discourse*. Notice that the speaking or the

2) singing is done by inspiration; this inspiration has to come from the Holy Spirit of God.

3) In *Proverbs 30:1* the word *massa* is used (pronounced mas-saw'); it comes from the root word nasa': It means *a burden, an utterance, tribute, mental desire*.

4) In *Daniel 9:24* the word nabiy' is used (pronounced *naw-bee'*); It comes from a root word naba' which means *a prophet or inspired man*.

5) In *Matthew 13:14* the word *propheteia* is used and it means *prediction*: It comes from a compound word which means *a foreteller*, an *inspired speaker, a poet*. Prophecy can come through *the spoken word, through poetry or through a song*. There is more to the prophetic than someone giving us a predictive word.

The Prophet

Prophets are individuals chosen by God to speak by Divine inspiration as oracles to reveal His instructions to His people and to warn individuals and nations about coming judgments if they do not repent. *"Where there is no vision, the people perish: but he that keepeth the law, happy is he"* The complete Jewish Bible translates it this way, *"Without a prophetic vision, the people throw off all restraint; but he who keeps Torah is happy (Proverbs 29:18)*. The Hebrew word for vision there is chazown (pronounced *khaw-zone*); it means *a dream, revelation, or an oracle*; it comes from the root word *chazah* (pronounced *khaw-zaw*); it means *to gaze at; mentally, to perceive*. Prophets receive mental pictures in the form of a vision or visions from God. This is evidenced by the words spoken by the Prophet Isaiah, *"In the year that King Uzziah died I saw also the Lord sitting upon a throne high and lifted up, and his train filled the temple"* (Isaiah 6:1).

Ezekiel declared, *"Now it came to pass in the thirtieth year, in the fourth month, in the fifth day of the month, as I was among the captives by the river of Chebar, that the heavens were opened, and I saw visions of God"* (*Ezekiel 1:1*). Before the prophet heard anything, he saw something. Habakkuk declared, *"I will stand upon my watch, and set me upon the tower, and will watch to see what he will say unto me, and what I shall answer when I am reproved"* (Habakkuk 2:1 KJV). God was going to speak and Habakkuk would see a picture of what was being spoken. Prophets are not just hearers, they are seers. The LORD asked Jeremiah, *"What seest thou"* (Jeremiah 1:11).

Paradigm Shift

Under the Old Testament paradigm, the Spirit of God would come upon certain individuals chosen by God like Deborah or Joel. These individuals were called prophets and they were used mightily by God to bring correction and instruction to His people and the surrounding nations.

Fidel Donaldson

When John the Baptist came on the scene to prepare the way for the Lord Jesus, there was a shift in the prophetic paradigm. Through Jesus' death, burial and resurrection, salvation would be available for anyone desiring to repent from sin and have faith in Him. An integral part of salvation includes the gift of the Holy Spirit and with the gift of the Spirit comes the ability to prophesy.

The Bible declares, *"God, who at sundry times and in diverse manners spake in time past unto the fathers by the prophets, hath in these last days spoken unto us by his Son, whom he hath appointed heir of all things, by whom also He made the worlds;" (Hebrews 1:1-2).* God is still speaking to His people prophetically, but now it is coming through His Son which the angel confirmed by the statement he made to John that *"the testimony of Jesus Christ is the spirit of prophecy."*

The Spirit and Prophecy

When we understand the dynamics of the relationship between the Spirit and prophecy, we get a clear understanding why Jesus told His disciples, *"I tell you the truth; It is expedient for you that I go away: for if I go not away, the Comforter will not come unto you; but if I depart, I will send him unto you" (John 16:7).* Besides reproving the world of sin, righteousness and judgment, the Spirit of truth would guide the disciples into all truth. He shall not speak of Himself, but He would speak the things that He heard. He will glorify Jesus and show the disciples things to come; I consider things to come prophetic things. Without the Spirit, Jesus will not be glorified in us, we will not know the things the Spirit has heard and we would be ignorant of things to come.

Praise Worship and the Spirit of Prophecy

When we yield to the leading of the Holy Spirit, we will experience those things which Jesus told His disciples would come when the Comforter came. Unlike Old Testament times, the Spirit was not coming for a visitation but a habitation. When we allow the Holy Spirit to take the lead, we will not be seduced by the enticing words of men's wisdom, will give us the ability to discern the authentic voice of God from the vain and the profane.

Not the Will of Man but the Holy Ghost

*"For we have not followed cunningly devised fables, when we made known unto you the power and coming of our Lord Jesus Christ, but were eyewitnesses of his majesty. For he received from God the Father honour and glory, when there came such a voice to him from the excellent glory, This is my beloved Son, in whom I am well pleased. And this voice which came from heaven we heard, when we were with him in the holy mount. We have also a more sure word of prophecy; whereunto ye do well that ye take heed, as unto a light that shineth in a dark place, until the day dawn, and the day star arise in your hearts: Knowing this first, that no prophecy of the scripture is of any private interpretation. For the prophecy came not in old time by the **will of man**: but **holy men of God spake** as they were **moved by the Holy Ghost**"* (2 Peter 1:16-21). Worship will cause the glory to manifest and out of the glory we will hear the prophetic voice. We cannot experience the glory without holiness and the Holy Ghost will not move us if we are not walking in holiness. Without holiness, people will prophesy out of their will and not from being moved by the Holy Ghost.

Fidel Donaldson

Prophecy should never come from the will of men motivated solely by monetary or some other personal gain. In the verses above we see another confirmation of the Holy Spirit and the prophetic. No matter how enticing a prophecy sounds, if it is not from the Holy Ghost, it is *pathetic* not *prophetic*. As children of God, we should be thankful for the individuals chosen by God to speak to His people prophetically, but we should also recognize the fact that through the power and indwelling presence of the Holy Ghost, God desires to speak through us and to speak to us prophetically. Some people get excited when a certain prophet comes to town because they hope he or she will call them out and give them a word. Some of them are willing to shell out large sums of money to bless the prophet, but there should be balance. I thank God for the ministry of the true prophet; if the prophet is not available we should be able to receive a word from the Lord. When we need a word from the Lord, we should find a place in worship to glorify God in the beauty of holiness, seek a moving of the Spirit and a well of prophecy will spring up in us. It does not matter that you don't have the title prophet in front of your name or you have not been ordained a prophet by someone; As long as you have the Holy Spirit living on the inside of you, worship God because the testimony of Jesus Christ is the Spirit of prophecy.

Praise Worship and the Spirit of Prophecy

PART THREE

Fidel Donaldson

Praise Worship and the Spirit of Prophecy

Chapter 7

Prophetic Manifestation

I remember a time when I needed five hundred dollars to take care of some business, but I did not have sufficient funds in the bank and did not desire to borrow or ask anyone for the money. I decided to go into my prayer room and set an atmosphere of worship. I put on some of my favorite worship songs and began to worship God. I stayed in the prayer room for a couple of hours in total worship. When my wife came home she stepped into the room with the mail in her hands; without hesitation I stuck out my hand and asked her emphatically, *"Is there a check in the mail for me,"* her response was, *"as a matter of fact there is."* She handed me two envelopes; one of them was a check from a business I was a part of so she knew that envelope contained a check, but there was another envelope that looked like a letter. When I opened the letter there was a check enclosed in the amount of five hundred dollars. When I tell people that I prophesy to my mail box concerning checks in the mail, some of them look at me with a strange look on their faces, but I do my best to maintain a constant posture of worship with an expectation that through the power of the Spirit, I can command the resources to come into my mail box because worship facilitates the prophetic in me. If Ezekiel could prophesy to dry bones and cause them to move, why can't I prophesy to my post office box, my mail box and my bank account?

The true prophetic voice comes from the Spirit in worship. Once we are in the Spirit, we should not hesitate to bring forth the prophetic boldly and we should be able to discern the prophetic word coming from the mouth of a true prophet of God.

Prophet or Profit

Peter went on to say, *"But there were false prophets also among the people, even as there shall be false teachers among you."* A whole book can be written about false prophets and false teachers. I call them PROFITS because they are not moved or motivated by the Holy Spirit but by money and materialism.

In *Acts 13:6* there is recorded a story of Paul and Barnabas' encounter with a false prophet and sorcerer named Bar-jesus when they went through the isle of Paphos. Bar-jesus was able to influence the spiritual and political atmosphere of that region because he connected himself with the deputy of that country. The Bible describes the deputy as a prudent man who called for Barnabas and Paul, and desired to hear the word of God. Although the false prophet was around him, he knew he needed more and was able to discern that Barnabas and Paul had the word of God. The false prophet opposed them because he wanted to turn the deputy away from the faith, and once the deputy came into the knowledge of Jesus Christ his connection to the deputy would be severed. Speaking under the influence of the Holy Spirit who had filled Paul, the apostle called the false prophet a child of the devil and an enemy of righteousness who sought to pervert the right ways of the Lord. When the Holy Spirit finished speaking through Paul, Bar-jesus was blind and sought someone to lead him by the hand. The deputy was able to witness a true move of God because of the Spirit of God flowing through His servant Paul.

Hirelings

Individuals whom God has chosen to operate in the office of the prophet have been given a greater measure of grace in that area; these individuals must constantly guard their hearts because of the magnitude of the gift of prophecy and the influence the prophet has over the people of God. The prophet must die to self daily and stay in constant worship because it is easy to drift into a place where the motive for prophesying becomes self aggrandizement and carnality.

In the book of Nehemiah, there is an example of prophets who hired themselves out to the enemies of God's work. When Sanballat and his cohort Tobiah realized they could not weaken the hands of Nehemiah and the workers through threats, nor scare them into stopping the work God called them to finish, they hired some prophets from Israel in hopes they would convince him to stop building the wall. An individual by the name of Shemaiah tried to convince Nehemiah to shut himself in the temple so the enemies of the work would not come and slay them in the night.

Fidel Donaldson

Nehemiah was a brave man and a man of great discernment. His response was, *"should such a man as I flee? And who is there, that, being as I am, would go into the temple to save his life? I will not go in. And, lo, I perceive that God had not sent him; but that he pronounced this prophecy against me: for Tobiah and Sanballat had hired him. Therefore was he hired, that I should be afraid, and do so, and sin, and that they might have for an evil report, that they might reproach me. My God, think thou upon Tobiah and Sanballat according to these their works, and on the prophetess Noadiah, and the rest of the prophets, that would have put me in fear. (Nehemiah 6:10-14 KJV).*

The Hebrew word for *perceived* as it is used in *Nehemiah 6:12* is *nakar;* and it means *to scrutinize, to look intently at.* In these last and evil days, we must test the spirit, scrutinize and look intently in-order to avoid being deceived. The adversary knows that his end is near, so he will use individuals inside and outside the church to hinder us from completing our assignment. Having exhausted much external devices to get us to abandon our assignment from God, he will seductively infiltrate local congregations and entice individuals of importance, in hopes of stopping the work. We can learn from Nehemiah's response to the prophet Shemaiah and his cohorts. Anyone or anything that is contrary to what God has called us to do must be disregarded.

Foolish Prophets

*"Son of man, prophesy against the prophets of Israel that prophesy, and say thou unto them that prophesy out of **their own hearts**, hear ye the word of the Lord; Thus saith the Lord God; Woe unto the*

Praise Worship and the Spirit of Prophecy

foolish prophets, that follow their own spirit, and have seen nothing" (Ezekiel 13:2-3).

Ezekiel was instructed by God to prophesy against the prophets who speak from these two areas:

- The heart of man

- The spirit of man

The heart speaks of man's intellect, his will and his emotions and prophecy should not come from these places. No matter how intellectual the person may be, no matter how much they say they are ministering from their heart or their spirit, we have to reject any and all prophecy that does not come from the Spirit of God. Many people have suffered great harm and financial distress because some "PROFIT" used a familiar spirit to deceive them into thinking they should give large amounts of money, jewelry and other expensive valuables to the "PROFIT' so they could release a word from the Lord. God told Ezekiel, *"They have seen vanity and lying divination, saying, The LORD saith: and the LORD hath not sent them: and they have made others to hope that they would confirm the word" (Ezekiel 13:6).*

According to *2 Kings Chapter 4*, the Shunamite woman was able to discern that Elisha was a holy man of God, and when her discernment kicked in she gave radically to sustain him. I encourage radical giving into the lives of God's true prophets once Spirit led discernment has revealed who they are.

Fidel Donaldson

When God used the Prophet Elisha to heal Naaman the leper, Elisha refused to take an offering from him. Prophecy should not be bought or sold; neither should prophetic messages be tailored to suck money out of desperate, gullible and unsuspecting people. As previously stated I believe in men and women of God being blessed and blessed tremendously, but I don't believe gifts from God ought to be used in a bewitching way for financial gain.

Ezekiel described so-called prophets that follow their own spirit as foolish and said they have seen nothing. Someone can come with a familiar spirit and say something that is accurate but is not of the Spirit of God. We have to be careful not to fall prey to this type of chicanery. True Spirit led worship will cause us to be sensitive to and discerning of the true voice of God. Once we know His voice, we will not be led astray by the seductive voice of the false, foolish prophet practicing sorcery and divination. King Saul was so desperate that instead of receiving a word from God through worship he decided to seek out the witch of Endor with a familiar spirit. How sad that the man who once prophesied when he was in the company of the prophets while they were worshipping, had fallen to such a low estate that he would seek out a witch to try to get a word from a dead prophet. He committed suicide on the battle field not long after when he was wounded by Philistine archers. We don't need the help of psychics, witches, warlocks or tarot card readers to know what will come to pass. We have the Holy Spirit and the word of God to give us instructions and directions. I thank God for grace because God told His prophet Moses, *"thou shalt not suffer a witch to live" (Exodus 22:18)*.

One Hundred Fold

When the Holy Spirit speaks to us and we are able to hear and obey Him, we will have a great testimony. A number of years ago I felt the Lord was leading me to convene a prayer gathering in New York City. I went to my friend Jose Vargas' house for him to book the ticket online for me because I did not have internet access at the time. While I was there, his daughter Jennifer was home and I clearly heard the Spirit tell me to write her a check for fifty dollars. My resources were extremely limited at the time, so in my mind I thought, since I am the one going to the New York, she and her dad should give me fifty dollars, of course I did not say that to them. I know it was the Holy Spirit because I had heard and obeyed His voice before and experienced the awesome results.

I wrote out the check and handed it to her, and when she looked at it she started to cry. Her dad told her to tell me why she was crying and she informed me that the rent check was late that month and they had finally received it, but did not have the late fee; the late fee was fifty dollars. The Holy Spirit had given me the exact amount she needed to cover the late fee and I am glad that I heard and obeyed because God would give me the increase in New York City.

The first service in New York was on a Friday and there weren't many people in attendance that night, but I learned that God does not need many people in attendance to manifest His glory. A lady came to me at the end of the service and introduced herself. She informed me that she had received salvation in Jacksonville, Florida where I lived. The next night, that same lady came to me and told me she had forgotten her check book and I told her it was ok; the next thing she said to me caused my eyes to enlarge and they are already big. She said, *"You don't understand, the Lord Just told me to write you a check for five thousand dollars."* I leaned forward, looked her right in the eyes and said, *"Excuse me, did you just say, "The Lord told you to write me a check for five thousand dollars," and she said, 'yes.'* The following day she invited my wife and me to her home and handed me an envelope with a check in it for five thousand dollars.

When the Holy Spirit speaks, He speaks clearly and specifically; the challenge for us is to make sure we are sensitive to His voice and have a spirit of obedience, especially when He asks us to do something that challenges our flesh. Fifty dollars may not sound like a lot of money, but when you are doing a meeting out of town and have to rent a hotel conference room, you need all the finances you can get. I sincerely believe that my obedience in releasing the fifty dollars was tied to the lady's obedience in releasing the five thousand. I know this because I found out later that she was not going to give any offering the first night because I had removed the drummer who played. During the praise and worship on Friday night, I could easily tell that the drummer was an amateur. He was clanging on the drums, so I went to his Bishop and told him the drummer was not getting the job done and he should be removed.

Praise Worship and the Spirit of Prophecy

As far as I was concerned, I had traveled too far and sacrificed too much to have the praise and worship messed up by the drummer. An out of town gathering is not the place for someone to play the drums that have not attained a high level of proficiency. The Bishop did not move, so I went to the drummer and took the drum sticks out of his hands. One of the attendees told me that as the drummer exited the room, he let out a few expletives; it was obvious that besides being a terrible drummer, he also had a cussing spirit. I knew that praise and worship was the key to what God wanted to do in those meetings, and I was not going to sit back and allow the enemy to sabotage it. The lady who gave me the five thousand dollars on Saturday night had taken out forty dollars to give in the offering that Friday, but put it back in her purse and told her prayer partner she was not going to give me anything after I took the sticks from the drummer. I found out later that she was a frequent visitor to the church the drummer attended. When the atmosphere in the room shifted and I shared my testimony, she realized I was not a mean person, just a servant seeking to glorify God.

It is never about embarrassing people, but in all things God must get the glory. When we come together to have an encounter with God, we must come with the knowledge that He is a God of excellence, and we should give Him our best. In our meetings, we must create an atmosphere of worship that is conducive to the entrance of the presence of God through His Spirit, and when we create that type of atmosphere, we will be able to receive from the riches that are in His glory. There are times when we will have to take the initiative and be bold in the Holy Ghost. We don't desire to hurt anyone's feelings, so we do it in a spirit of meekness and humility. At the end of the day, it is all about the presence of God and not people. *"In His presence there is fullness of joy and at His right hand there are pleasures for evermore"* (Psalm 16:11).

Praise Worship and the Spirit of Prophecy

Chapter 8

Your Sons and Your Daughters Shall Prophesy

My daughter Makeda works for a credit card company and wanted to apply for a position when the company started a mortgage division. The supervisor in her division told her and other co-workers not to apply for the position because the position required experience. When I spoke with Makeda, I told her if she did not apply, the answer was definitely no so she should apply. She decided to apply for the position and was hired for the position. When she started training, she saw the supervisor who told her team not to apply in training for the same position. After a few months in her new position, Makeda came to me and told me that she was number one in her department and was getting a nice bonus for being number one. When the Holy Spirit is on the inside of a person, He will supply the wisdom needed to secure a certain position. We should not allow people to talk us out of applying for something because of a lack of experience, because training is usually provided and if the interview process goes well the prospective employer will hire you and train you despite the lack of experience.

Pentecost Power

On the Day of Pentecost, the New Testament Church of the Lord Jesus Christ was established when One Hundred and Twenty believers assembled in an upper room and received the baptism of the Holy Ghost. Prior to the outpouring of the Holy Ghost, Jesus had assembled with them and commanded them to tarry at Jerusalem until they were endued with power from on High. Prior to the baptism of the Holy Ghost, baptism was an outward sign of an individuals desire to be cleansed from sin and be reconciled to God; with the baptism of the Holy Ghost the emphasis was on an inward work that the Spirit would perform in the life of the believer so he or she could become a temple or a dwelling place for the Holy Spirit.

Forty days after His resurrection and ten days after His ascension, the promise was fulfilled as the one hundred and twenty believers were assembled in the upper room in prayer and supplication. There were males and females in that room, and they were on one accord in a spirit of unity and oneness. On that day, they received the great and precious gift of the Holy Ghost when cloven tongues of fire sat upon each of them and they began to speak with other tongues as the Spirit gave them utterance. This was the initial manifestation of the Holy Ghost, but not the only manifestation.

When the Holy Ghost is poured out on an individual, along with tongues there should be fruit like love, joy, peace, longsuffering, gentleness, goodness, faith, meekness, and temperance; there should also be the manifestation of the Spirit in the form of, the word of wisdom, the word of knowledge, the gifts of healing, the working of miracles, discerning of spirits, interpretation of tongues and prophecy. In charismatic Pentecostal meetings, I expect to hear a great deal about the baptism of the Holy Ghost with the evidence of speaking in other tongues, but I also expect to hear about the fruit and the gifts of

Praise Worship and the Spirit of Prophecy

the same Spirit. Prophecy is one of those gifts, and it should be prominent in the lives of disciples and in our meetings.

On the Day of Pentecost, Peter stood up with the eleven to minister the first sermon of the young church; in response to the questions asked by the devout Jews gathered at Jerusalem Peter quoted from the Prophet Joel, *"And it shall come to pass in the last days, saith God, I will pour out of my Spirit upon all flesh: and your sons and your daughters shall prophesy, and your young men shall see visions, and your old men shall dream dreams: And on my servants and on my handmaidens I will pour out in those day of my Spirit; and they shall prophesy"* (Acts 2:17-18). With this scripture in mind, it is safe to say that the last days will not only be marked by earthquakes in diverse places, wars and rumors of war, but also by a great outpouring of God's Spirit which will be evidenced by prophecy, dreams and visions.

A Noise a shaking and a Coming Together

By quoting the prophet Joel, Peter confirms for the New Testament Church the connection between the Spirit and prophecy. The said connection is confirmed in other places in the Bible. In *Ezekiel 37* the story is told of the valley of dried bones and in that story we see the moving of the Spirit and the command to prophesy. Ezekiel declared, *"The hand of the Lord was upon me, and carried me out in the **spirit** of the Lord, and set me down in the midst of the valley which was full of bones."* God asked Ezekiel if the bones could live, then told him to, *"**Prophesy** upon these bones and say unto them, O ye dry bones,* *hear the word of the Lord."* In *verse 7* Ezekiel said, *"So I prophesied as I was commanded: and as I prophesied, there was a noise and behold a shaking, and the bones came together, bone to his bone."*

When we are in the Spirit of the Lord and we prophesy as God commands, there will be a sound released, a shaking and a coming together. *"Bone to his bone"* represents order and structure. When the true prophetic word comes, it will bring order and it will bring structure; things will begin to line up and they will begin to flow. When Ezekiel prophesied under the unction of the Holy Spirit, the bones came together but there was no breath in them. Since there was no breath, there was no life in them. Job declared, *"The Spirit of God hath made me, and the breath of the Almighty hath given me life"* (*Job 33:4*). The same *ruach* or breath that gave life to Job caused the dry bones to live.

Dead things can come to life through the Spirit via a prophetic word from the Lord spoken through the mouths of his servants. The widow of Zarephath was in the midst of famine, down to her last meal which she was ready to prepare for herself and her son before they starved to death, until Elijah spoke a prophetic word which caused her meal barrel and oil to multiply. When creditors were beating down the door of a widow of one of the sons of the prophets and she went to Elisha for help, he asked her what she had in the house. She told the prophet all she had in the house was a pot of oil. Such great revelation there; oil represents the Holy Spirit and we are the house where the oil

Praise Worship and the Spirit of Prophecy

is located; through prophetic instructions from the prophet the widow who was deluged by creditors one moment became debt free and an oil distributor in her community.

Elisha caused the dead womb of the Shunamite woman to come to life through a prophetic word; through a prophetic word he was able to warn her of the famine that would come upon the land for seven years *(2 Kings 4:17 and chapter 8 respectively)*.

The Spirit has not been poured out on all flesh yet, but if you are a child of God, born again, washed in the Blood of Jesus, and have His Spirit, whether you are a son, daughter, a servant or a handmaiden, you should see visions, should dream dreams, and you should prophesy. A prophetic word from the child of God can cause a shaking, a moving and a coming together. Don't allow the spirit of fear to hinder you from bringing forth the prophetic word when you feel the unction of the Spirit. When you are in a dry place, prophesy life, when things around you appear to be stagnant, prophesy life. Prophesy as God commands and there will be manifestation.

If we refuse to speak like the prophet Jeremiah did when he faced persecution, God's word will become like fire shut up in our bones. Remember, when the Holy Ghost came on the day of Pentecost there was a sound, and there was cloven tongues like fire. God has not given us the precious gift of the Holy Spirit for us to be one dimensional. With the Holy Ghost, He has given us the dunamis power to move and shake things. Don't use your tongue to speak doubt, use it to bring forth a prophetic word that will facilitate change and transformation. Anyone can speak the problem, but who is willing to prophesy the solution? When Belazeel was chosen by God to build the tabernacle, the LORD spoke these words to Moses, *"And I have filled him with the spirit of God, in wisdom, and in understanding, and in knowledge, and in all manner of workmanship (Exodus 31:2).* It is interesting that Bezaleel was from the tribe of Judah, and as previously stated Judah means praise. There is more to the Holy Spirit than tongues; tongues were the initial evidence of the baptism of the Holy Ghost on the day of Pentecost, but when you search the scriptures you see other manifestations of the spirit and one of them is the ability to prophesy. The manifestation of the Holy Spirit is multifaceted and we must embrace all that He has to offer us.

The Gift of Tongues and Some

The same Spirit who is manifested in fruit, wisdom, tongues and gifts, will speak through us prophetically if we do not quench Him out of fear. There are places we will go, people we will visit and God may want to use us to speak prophetically to someone and we must not allow fear to cripple us because someone did not ordain us a prophet, or we fell we may miss and get it wrong; it is not about us but about the fact that God desires to speak through us. The Spirit of God will lead us like he did Ezekiel into places that are dry because He wants us to prophesy life over those places.

The key to the prophecy spoken by Joel and quoted by Peter is the gift of the Spirit. Sinners are outside of the covenant God established with Abraham, so God sent His only begotten son Jesus to shed His blood for the remission of sin so the sinner can repent and receive the promise of the Spirit. God promised Abraham that in him would all the families of the earth be blessed, but the blessing cannot be received with a nature permeated and saturated with sin.

In his letter to the Galatians, the Apostle Paul sheds light on this promise when he wrote, *"Christ hath redeemed us from the curse of the law, being made a curse for us: for it is written, Cursed is every one that hangeth on a tree: That the blessing of Abraham might come on the Gentiles through Jesus Christ; that we might receive the promise of the Spirit through faith"* (Galatians 3:13-14).

The greatest blessing an individual can receive is to be washed in the Blood of Jesus and have the Spirit of God dwelling on the inside. The Holy Spirit will not dwell in temples that are not redeemed and the Blood of Jesus is the only thing that can cleanse our temple so the Spirit can reside there. You can see how precious the gift of the Spirit is by the sacrifice made by Jesus for us to receive Him. If you are reading this book, and you have not received Jesus into your heart, this is a good time to take a moment and ask Him to forgive you of your sins, to be the Lord of your life and to fill you with the Holy Spirit.

Fidel Donaldson

Chapter 9

The Minstrel and the Prophet

Prior to reading about the story of an encounter that the Prophet Elisha had with the King of Israel and Jehoshaphat the King of Judah, I was not very knowledgeable of the ministry of the minstrel and its correlation to the prophetic. I thought a minstrel was just someone who played an instrument. My understanding was enlightened once I was able to glean from the story told in *2 Kings Chapter 3.*

The events took place after Ahab was dead and the king of Moab rebelled against the king of Israel. The Bible declares, *"And king Jehoram went out of Samaria the same time, and numbered all Israel"* *(2 Kings 3:11).* From the outset, it is evident that the king of Israel is putting his trust in numbers and not God. I know people say, "There is strength in numbers," and I understand the point they are making, but if God is not in the numbers then it does not matter how large the numbers are. When David numbered Israel before a particular battle, it brought judgment upon the people. While we must always take an honest assessment of our troops' strength, we must understand that it is God, who gives us the victory in Christ Jesus and not the strength of our numbers.

Praise Worship and the Spirit of Prophecy

After he made his count, the king of Israel sent to Jehoshaphat, the king of Judah and solicited his help in the battle. Jehoshaphat is the king of Judah, and Judah is the tribe that led the way when the children of Israel were on the move. Praise and worship should always lead the way for us. There is some very important language used by Jehoram and Jehoshaphat. Jehoram said this to Jehoshaphat, *"the king of Moab hath rebelled against me: wilt thou go with me against Moab to battle?* Jehoshaphat responded by saying, *"I will go up."* Judah must go up, for when the praises go up, the blessings come down. Jehoram needed him to go with him but Jehoshaphat knew that the way to victory was upward.

The way up was through the wilderness of Edom, and they were joined by the king of Edom. At a certain point in their journey they came to a dry place and there wasn't any water for them or their cattle. Once again the king of Israel showed a lack of trust in the God and began to complain and speak defeat. *"But Jehoshaphat said, is there not here a prophet of the Lord, that we may inquire of the LORD by him" (2 Chronicles 3:11)?* Beloved, on your way up, you may encounter a wilderness, a dry place where it appears the Spirit of the Lord is not moving. Please do not adopt a posture of murmuring and complaining, because God does not inhabit the murmuring and complaining of His people, He inhabits their praise. If we are not careful, we can cause ourselves to be at a disadvantage because of the words we speak out of our mouths. When you are going into battle, make sure you are surrounded by people who trust God and walk by faith not by sight.

Jehoshaphat understood the power of the prophetic word coming from the mouth of a truth prophet, so instead of speaking out of a place of fear and a lack of trust in God, he inquired about a prophet of the Lord. *"And one of the king of Israel's servants answered and said, Here is Elisha the son of Shaphat, which poured water on the hands of Elijah" (2 Chronicles 3:11).* It is important to take notice of the manner in which the servant described Elisha. He did not describe him by title first, or talk about the fact that he had the double portion of Elijah's Spirit, but made mention of the fact that he *"poured water on the hands of Elijah."* In other words, he highlighted the fact the he had served the prophet Elijah. Pouring water on the hands of another for washing was a servant's work; Elisha had been Elijah's minister in the same way Joshua was Moses' minister.

Are people hanging around you as a ministry gift because they are looking for a position, or are they doing it because they desire to be mentored through servant-hood? Check the spirit of the armourbearer and make sure it isn't the spirit of a pallbearer.

It is such a shame that it took the servant of the king of Israel to let them know that the prophet Elisha was in the vicinity. Jehoram should have known that there was a true prophet there, but he was used to being around prophets who told him what he wanted to hear and not, *"thus saith the Lord."*

Praise Worship and the Spirit of Prophecy

Praise and worshippers know the true prophetic voice from the voice of the false prophet because they spend time in the presence of the Lord through worship and can discern when He is speaking through His servants the prophets. *"And Jehoshaphat said, the word of the LORD is with him"* (2 Chronicles 3:12). This should be one of our greatest desires that someone would say concerning us, "The word of the LORD is with him."

When they arrived at the place where Elisha dwelt, he was not happy to see Jehoram the king of Israel, because he knew the history of the relationship both he and his fore parents had with idolatry and false prophets through the introduction of Baal worship to the nation of Israel. *"And Elisha said, As the LORD of hosts liveth, before whom I stand, surely, were it not that I regard the presence of Jehoshaphat the king of Judah, I would not look toward thee, nor see thee"* (2 Chronicles 3:14).

Prophets like Elijah and Elisha were zealous for the LORD and did not tolerate idolatry and false prophets. He respected Jehoshaphat because he knew Jehoshaphat was a king who feared the LORD. The greater our position in God the more circumspect we should walk in order to not become a stumbling block to others and cause a reproach against the name of the LORD.

Fidel Donaldson

Bring Me a Minstrel

Elisha served the prophet Elijah faithfully and received a double portion of his spirit when he was taken up to heaven. He did twice the miracles of Elijah before he left the earth. I mention this because, before he starts to give a prophetic word to the three kings, he asked for a minstrel to be brought to him. Here is one of the most awesome scripture connecting the importance of the sound of worship and the sound of the prophetic.

The Hebrew word for minstrel is *nagan* (pronounced *naw-gan*); it means *a player on instruments, to sing to stringed instruments, make melody or to make music.* We all may not be able to play a stringed instrument, but all of us can make a joyful noise unto the Lord; we can all make melody in our hearts to the Lord. It may sound off key to people in the natural but God receives it if it is done in the Spirit and comes through a dedicated heart.

When the minstrel played, the hand of the LORD came upon Elisha and he began to prophesy and give instructions to the three kings. We need the hand of the Lord to come upon the minstrels responsible for leading us into His presence as we congregate for His glory. We don't need a sound that will entertain our souls to the exclusion of the prophetic voice from heaven. We don't need minstrels who are trying to showcase their gifts and talents for accolades and materialistic opportunity. We need minstrels like David who are panting for the presence of the Lord like the deer pants for the water brook.

Once the minstrels set the atmosphere in our gathering, the Spirit of prophecy will flow profusely and prolifically. As the congregants come in unity to the sound being made by the minstrels, making melody in their hearts before the Lord, God will begin to prophesy to them and through them right in the midst of the congregation. I don't believe for a moment that God desires to prophesy exclusively to and through the individual that is called to the office of the prophet. Moses was a great prophet and he desired that God would prophesy through all His people.

Eldad and Medad

The scriptures record a particular meeting when the LORD came down in a cloud and spoke to Moses. After speaking to him, he tookthe spirit that was on Moses and gave it to the seventy elders. *"And it came to pass, that, when the spirit rested upon them, they prophesied, and did not cease" (Numbers 11:25).* It is important that the people in and around the leader has his or her spirit. We know that we must have the Spirit of God, but the Bible did not say, God took His Spirit and put it on the seventy elders, but that he took the spirit that rested on Moses, and we know Moses had God's Spirit because of his face to face communion with God. If the people around you do not have your spirit for the mandate the Lord has given you, there will be a spirit of sedition, a spirit of Absalom and a spirit of Ananias and Sapphira in the camp.

Fidel Donaldson

Two individuals by the name of Eldad and Medad remained in the camp when God was meeting with Moses at the tabernacle. Eldad and Medad prophesied in the camp. They were not out of order because the Bible informs us that the spirit rested on them. The same spirit from Moses that was given to the seventy elders causing them to prophesy rested on the two men causing *them* to prophesy. When two young men ran and told Moses, and Moses' minister, Joshua wanted Moses to stop them. Moses asked Joshua if he was envious of the situation for his sake. Moses then responded with this emphatic statement: *"would God that all the LORD's people were prophets, and that the LORD would put his spirit upon them! (Numbers 11:29).* This was not just a whimsical wish on the part of Moses, because, when the comforter came on the day of Pentecost to endue the disciples with Holy Ghost power, with Him came the ability to prophesy in the Spirit.

Prophetic Protocol

When true Spirit led worship reaches a certain level in the congregation, the people of God should be allowed to come forth with a prophetic word, but their coming forth must be in order and decency. I must state again unequivocally and emphatically that this must be done in order and in decency because God is not the author of confusion. I was in a prophetic convocation at The Worship Place recently and the speaker was Prophetess Tonya Hall. During her teaching, she referenced *1 Corinthians 14:29-33* where Paul instructed the church at Corinth to, *"Let the prophets speak two or three, and let the other judge. If any thing be revealed to another that sitteth by, let*

Praise Worship and the Spirit of Prophecy

the first hold his peace. For ye may all prophesy one by one, that all may learn, and all may be comforted. And the spirits of the prophets are subject to the prophets. For God is not the author of confusion, but of peace, as in all churches of the saints." Prophetess Hall said, *"Paul set up a system for the prophetic."* It was a system of prophetic protocol and if we follow it there will not be confusion in the midst. We cannot allow the spirit of fear of losing control to cause us to stifle or shutdown the prophetic voice of God that desires to come forth through His people in the midst of Spirit led worship. When we plug into the system, the system will work for us.

The ministry of the minstrel and the prophetic are evident throughout the scriptures and in some cases, the prophet or prophetess flowed prophetically and as a minstrel simultaneously. After the defeat of Pharaoh's army at the Red Sea, Moses and the children of Israel sang a song unto the LORD. *"And Miriam the prophetess, the sister of Aaron, took a timbrel in her hand; and all the women went out after her with timbrels and with dances. And Miriam answered them, Sing ye to the LORD, for he hath triumphed gloriously; the horse and his rider hath he thrown into the sea"* (Exodus 15:20-21). This is a picture we need to see in our services and when we do I believe we gain greater victories over our enemies. The leader or leaders of the local assembly should actively participate in the worship experience and be seen singing and dancing before the Lord like Moses, Miriam, and David.

Fidel Donaldson

PART FOUR

Fidel Donaldson

Chapter 10

Is Saul Among the Prophets?

The Prophet Samuel was a great man of God who was dedicated to God by his mother Hannah from childhood. He served the Lord and His people faithfully well into his old age and appointed his two sons to be judges over Israel when it was time for him to step down; unfortunately ministry is not a family business, and there are times when the children do not have the same reverence for God like their parents. This was the case with Samuel's two sons, Joel and Abiah. They took bribes and perverted judgment so the elders of Israel came to Samuel and told him they wanted a king to rule over them like the other nations because of the actions of his sons.

In seeking to be like the nations, Israel was rejecting God's theocratic governance. They were to be a peculiar people unto Him, not a people resembling the other nations. God instructed Samuel to anoint Saul to be Israel's first king. God has such a unique way of connecting people for His purpose. Saul left home with a servant to search for his father's donkeys and was instructed by his servant about an honorable man of God who could help them.

Praise Worship and the Spirit of Prophecy

The High Place

Through Spirit led worship, prophets are able to go to a high place where they receive the word of the Lord for the people. In 1 Samuel Chapters 9 and 10, we see a great portrait of this process painted by words. Saul and his servant have to go up a hill to get to the prophet Samuel. On their way up the hill, they encountered two young maidens going out to draw water and inquired of them the whereabouts of Samuel. The maidens told them Samuel had come to the city because there was a sacrifice of the people that day in the high place. It takes a sacrifice to get to the high place to receive prophetically from the presence of God. On their way up to the high place, they encounter Samuel who instructs them to go up before him to the high place because they would eat with him for two days, and then Samuel would release them and tell Saul all that was in his heart. After letting Saul know that the donkeys were found, Samuel ministered to him and anointed his head with oil to be the next ruler of Israel. Samuel gives specific instructions on what would happen as he departed and headed down from the high place to return home.

A Company of Prophets

Saul would experience three signs which would further confirm to him and the people his divine call and commission.

1: he would meet two men near Rachel's tomb at Zelzah on the border of Benjamin and Ephraim, who would tell him of the whereabouts of the lost donkeys;

2: he would meet three men at the (oak) tree of Tabor, somewhere between Zelzah and Gibeah, who would give him two loaves of bread;

3: he would meet a company of prophets descending from the high place at Gibeah.

Samuel told him the company of prophets coming down from the high place would have a *psaltery*, and a *tabret*, and a *pipe*, and a *harp*, before them; and they would prophesy. The modus operandi for experiencing the prophetic individually or corporately has not changed.

It is important to note where the prophets were coming from and what was before them. This is one of the strongest confirmations in scripture of worship, the Spirit and prophecy. The symbolism and the imagery of worship and the prophetic are incredible. Notice that the instruments of worship are before the prophets. Every God-ward action that we undertake must be prefaced by worship.

Worship will take us to the high place, and once we get there, the Spirit of prophecy will flow. True prophets spend a great deal of time in the high place in the presence of God with intense worship. I have never met a true prophet of God who was not passionate about worship, and I have never met a passionate worshipper who was not prophetic. Once an individual gets in an atmosphere of worship like Saul did when he encountered the company of prophets, transformation and change are inevitable. *"And the Spirit of the Lord will come upon thee, and thou shalt prophesy with them, and shalt be*

Praise Worship and the Spirit of Prophecy

turned into another man" (1 Samuel 10:6). In these verses we see Worship, the Spirit of the LORD and the prophetic. This is the central message of this book.

Saul could not prophesy until the Spirit of the Lord came upon Him. The Spirit of the LORD did not manifest until the company of prophets came down from the high place with the instruments of worship before them. Saul was not a prophet but association with participation brings manifestation. I have no doubt that Saul joined in the euphoric worship, causing the Spirit of the Lord to rest upon him. Once the Spirit rested on him, he was turned into another man. Worship will cause the Spirit of God to rest on us and once He rests on us, change and transformation will manifest.

I believe we can experience what Saul experienced in our meetings today, but in-order to have that experience we must have the same atmosphere that he encountered. When we congregate and are led to the high place in worship, we should have an expectation that the Spirit of God will rest on us and we will prophesy and be changed. Many people would love to prophesy, but I love the fact that the Spirit also changes us. Can you imagine leaving your home to look for something that is lost and returning home prophesying, transformed and receiving an anointing to be a king? One moment you are with a servant, the next moment you are being anointed by a great honorable man of God for your Divine assignment, and the next moment you are in the company of prophets prophesying! God is an awesome God!

Fidel Donaldson

The people who knew Saul were astonished when they heard him prophesying, *"And it came to pass, when all that knew him before time saw that, behold, he prophesied among the prophets, then the people said one to another, What is this that is come unto the son of Kish? Is Saul also among the prophets" (1 Samuel 10:11)?*

When we have had a true encounter of the prophetic kind by the Spirit of God through worship, people will see and hear the change and transformation that has taken place. Birds of a feather flock together, so, if you desire to prophesy and have a life transforming encounter through the Spirit; get in a place and posture of deep worship and surround yourself with like minded people who love intense profuse and prolific worship. You can set the tone of the atmosphere where you are with a posture of worship. There are times when we allow our atmosphere to determine our mood and our disposition in a negative way, but that should be the other way around. We may find ourselves in an environment or atmosphere that is not conducive to peace and joy, but we should not allow that to cause our mood to be one of melancholy, but instead we should turn that atmosphere into one of worship and expect a shift to take place. When you have God's Holy Spirit on the inside, you have the power to be an atmosphere changer.

Praise Worship and the Spirit of Prophecy

Where are you today? What type of mood are you in? Is your environment a fortified prison, a nursing home or a physically debilitated body that has you feeling trapped? Is it an emotional prison caused by despair and depression? John the Baptist was a mighty prophet of God, but when he was in prison facing death, he began to question the identity of Jesus. Intense worship will transform the atmosphere of your heart and your mind and change your disposition. You may not have the power to open the prison door, but like Paul and Silas when they were in the inner prison with their feet fastened with stocks, you can bring the presence of God into your sphere by **replacing pity with praise**, and **worry with worship**. When your sphere is changed, it will affect the people around you because they will see the change that has taken place in your life through the Spirit.

It is not easy to break forth in praise and worship when you are feeling down and depressed, but it is imperative that you press into that place and resist that spirit of oppression and depression that seek to keep you trapped in a dark place. To quote Minister Tassel Daley, "When I feel like praising Him, I will praise Him; When I don't feel like praising Him, I will praise Him. My praise is not based on my feelings; it is based on my obedience. Let everything that has breath, Praise the Lord." As you worship God in that place, His light will begin to dispel the darkness and will speak prophetically to you and through you by His Spirit. You must initiate the action; once you do that, God will do what He alone can do. The Spirit of God on the inside of you is greater than anything on the outside, so don't allow demonic spirits to control your environment. The enemy loves to keep us in a place of despondency and despair when things don't appear to be going in our favor, but we must remember the wells of salvation that is on the inside of us through the Holy Spirit. Heed the instructions given to us in the Bible by the prophet Isaiah, *"Therefore with joy shall ye draw water out of the wells of salvation. And in that day shall ye say, Praise the LORD, call upon his name, declare his doings among the people, make mention that his name is exalted. Sing unto the LORD; for he hath done excellent things: this is known in all the earth. Cry out and shout, thou inhabitant of Zion: for great is the Holy One of Israel in the midst of thee"* (Isaiah 12:3-6).

Praise Worship and the Spirit of Prophecy

Chapter 11

Worship Is My Prophetic Weapon

I never understood the revelation of worship as a prophetic weapon until I read the story of Jehoshaphat and his defeat of Moab Ammon and mount Seir. The story which is told in *2 Chronicles 20* is a story I love to read, because once again, it solidifies the connection between worship, the Spirit of the Lord and the prophetic word. An attack was launched against Judah by Moab Ammon and some of their confederates from mount Seir. When Jehoshaphat received the word that a great multitude was coming against Judah, he sought the Lord and called for a fast.

The enemy knows that the joy of the Lord is our strength, so he always seeks to sap our strength with attacks that try to overwhelm us. The enemy knows when Judah goes up, his attack will be thwarted, so he will attempt to shut it down. Whenever we are faced with a battle, Judah must be first and Judah must go up. *"Now after the death of Joshua it came to pass, that the children of Israel asked the LORD, saying, Who shall go up for us against the Canaanites first, to fight against them? And the LORD said, Judah shall go up: behold, I have delivered the land into his hand" (Judges 1:1-2).*

In the midst of their fasting, praying and the impending attack from their enemies, Jehoshaphat and all of Judah sought the LORD in prayer. There was a spirit of unity and oneness and that spirit of unity and oneness facilitated a prophetic word from the LORD. While the King and all the people were seeking the LORD in prayer, the Spirit of the LORD came upon a Levite of the sons of Asaph by the name of Jahaziel. The Spirit of the LORD did not rest on just anyone in the congregation but on a worshipper. Jahaziel had worship in his Genes because his forefather Asaph was a Levite; one of the leaders of David's choir *(1 Chronicles 6:39)*. He is mentioned along with David as skilled in music, and a "seer" *(2 Chronicles 29:30)*. In those days, a prophet was also called a seer. With that type of pedigree and stock, it is no surprise that the Spirit of the LORD would rest on Jahaziel and he would prophesy.

The Battle Belongs to God

He told all Judah, the inhabitants of Jerusalem, and King Jehoshaphat, *"Thus saith the LORD unto you, Be not afraid nor be dismayed by reason of this great multitude; for the battle is not yours, but God's" (2 Chronicles 20:15).* David uttered the same words when the giant Goliath came against Israel. David declared, *"And all this assembly shall know that the LORD saveth not with sword and spear: for the battle is the LORD's, and he will give you into our hands" (1 Samuel 17:47).* Beloved are you stressing at the moment because you are trying to fight battles from enemies that have come against your finances, your health, your marriage or your ministry? Are you trying to do it in your own strength when the battle belongs to God? You have a covenant with God through the Blood of Jesus and when that covenant was established through your born again experience, your enemies became God's enemies. Cast your cares upon him because He cares for you.

The prophetic word came as a weapon through the mouth of Jahaziel instructing them when they should go out against the enemy, and what the exact position of the enemy was. There is no better reconnoiter than the Spirit of the Lord. *The word reconnoiter means: to inspect, observe, or survey (an enemy position, strength, etc.) in order to gain information for military purposes.* After giving them the location of the enemy, he gave them the strategy for victory. Jahaziel told them they would not have to fight in that battle and they should not be afraid or dismayed because the LORD was with them. The enemy's tactic is to send a blitz against us like He did Job so fear and dismay can cripple and paralyze us. Judah would not need conventional methods of warfare to defeat the enemy because God was on their side and He never loses a battle.

No matter the size of the enemy that has come against you today, know assuredly that God is with you, and you and God are a majority, Find a place in worship, and wait for the prophetic voice from God that will give you the strategy for victory. Do not allow fear to paralyze you and put you in a position where the enemy can defeat you. No matter how insurmountable the odds may seem, wait on the Lord, be of good courage and He shall strengthen your heart!

I absolutely love Jehoshaphat and the people's posture after receiving the word from the Lord, *"And Jehoshaphat bowed his head with his face to the ground: and all Judah and the inhabitants of*

Jerusalem fell before the LORD, worshipping the LORD" (2 Chronicles 20:18). That is such a wonderful picture of the posture of *Shachah* and *Proskuneo*; a willingness to prostrate oneself before almighty Yahweh. Jehoshaphat was king, but like his forefather David before him he had no problem bowing before Father God in worship. We need leaders in the church who are willing to lay prostrate in the presence of our heavenly Father.

When the king bowed before God in worship, the Levites, the children of the Kohathites, and the children of the Korhites, stood up and praised the LORD God of Israel with a loud voice on high. These men were the descendants of the tabernacle musicians whom David appointed from the three Levitical families. As modern day priests and Levites who are part of the Judah priesthood, our temples must be filled with music for the Lord.

Jehoshaphat and the people rose early in the morning and headed towards the wilderness of Tekoa. As they went forth, Jehoshaphat stood and said, *"Hear me, O Judah, and ye inhabitants of Jerusalem; Believe in the LORD your God, so shall ye be established: believe his prophets, so shall ye prosper"* (*2 Chronicles 20:20*). He gave the people that word because he wanted to reassure them as they went to meet the enemy that God was with them, and He confirmed it through His prophets.

After consulting with the people, the king does something interesting. He did not get with the archers or the individuals that had the weapons, instead he appointed singers unto the LORD that should praise the beauty of holiness. (Interesting but effective battle strategy based on the word from the LORD given to them by Jahaziel.) The singers went before the army because praise and worship must always be first. Another example of the appointing of singers is found during the rebuilding of the temple,

"And when the builders laid the foundation of the temple of the LORD, they set the priests in their apparel with trumpets, and the Levites the sons of Asaph with cymbals, to praise the LORD, after the ordinance of David king of Israel. And they sang together by course in praising and giving thanks unto the LORD; because he is good, for his mercy endureth for ever toward Israel. And all the people shouted with a great shout, when they praised the LORD, because the foundation of the house of the LORD was laid" (Ezra 3:10)

If it's not broken, don't fix it; Jehoshaphat and Judah knew the power of praise because God had responded to His people's praise and worship on numerous occasions. "As they went before the army they said, *"Praise the LORD; for his mercy endureth for ever."* While they sang and praised, the LORD set ambushments against the children of Ammon, Moab, and mount Seir. Praise and worship will send confusion into the camp of our enemies and cause them to be ambushed. When the spirit of confusion came into the camp of the enemy, they began to attack one another. Not one of the enemies of Judah was allowed to escape, and not one person from Judah was lost because they obeyed the prophetic word from Jahaziel and saw the salvation of the LORD that was with them. Salvation does not only mean being saved from sin so we can go to heaven; it also means God will fight our battles when enemies come against us.

To the Victor Goes the Spoil

When Jehoshaphat and the people went to the watch tower in the wilderness, they saw many dead bodies and among the bodies were riches and precious jewels. There were so much jewels and riches; it took them three days to gather it together. On the fourth day they assembled themselves in the valley of *Berrachah* and there they blessed the LORD. When they were finished, they headed back to Jerusalem to the house of the LORD with psalteries and harps and trumpets.

They headed to the battle with worship, and once victory was won they returned with worship. Whenever we face a battle, we must face it with worship, and once the battle is over we must continue in worship.

When Praises go Up

Out of a deep committed place of worship will flow manifestations from the presence of God. Once I learned the importance of praise and worship, I always endeavor to stay in that posture. Several years ago I needed to have copies of my book *Perceive And Receive* printed, and had to go to a local printer because the date for the book release was rapidly approaching. I went to see a local printer on a Saturday, and he informed me that the cost would be higher than normal because the price of ink went up. In my mind, I thought about the fact that when praises go up blessings come down. When we adopt the *Matthew 6:33* principle of seeking the kingdom first and all its righteousness, we should expect the things we need to be added to us. How do we seek the kingdom?

Worship is one of the keys in seeking the kingdom. The Greek word for seek as it is used there is the word *zeteo* and it means to worship. Remember, God supplies all our needs according to His riches in glory by Christ Jesus, we must maintain a posture of worship which takes us into the glory so we can receive the riches.

The printer said I needed $1,000.00 which was not readily available, but I knew it was in the riches in the glory by Christ Jesus, so with boldness I told the printer I would return Monday. I spoke the word by faith and did not doubt in my heart. I had to preach at Narrow Way Ministries that Sunday and the Holy Spirit gave me a message on the word of faith. When I finished preaching and left the podium, a lady in the church walked up to me and placed a piece of paper in my hand; without looking at it I placed it in my pocket and went outside. While I was outside, I decided to look at the paper, and when I did I saw that it was a check for $1,000.00. I went to the sister the following week and told her about the need that I had to get the book printed and she explained to me that the Lord spoke to her that morning and told her to write me a check. When she inquired as to the amount, He told her He would show it to her during church service. While I was ministering the word of God, the Holy Spirit gave her the exact amount I needed without her even knowing that I needed it. Praise and worship will cause a moving of the Spirit and facilitate a prophetic word and a manifestation from the kingdom of God.

Chapter 12

New Testament Prophecy

In *1 Corinthians 14:3* Paul told the church, *"But he that prophesieth speaketh unto men to*

- *Edification*

- *Exhortation*

- *Comfort."*

Prophecy is one of the nine spiritual gifts given to the church by the Lord Jesus and it should be embraced and should manifest in all church gatherings. Once again it must be stated emphatically and equivocally that the ministry of the prophet and the gift of prophecy should be resident in our church gatherings. In his first letter to the Corinthian Church, the Apostle Paul wrote that Prophecy is a gift of the Spirit given to the church by grace. The Apostle did not want the church to be ignorant when it came to Spiritual gifts such as prophecy. If we as Disciples of Christ would search the scriptures diligently, God will bless us with wisdom knowledge and understanding concerning prophecy and other Spiritual gifts. Paul told them they were led by dumb idols when they were gentiles.

The Corinthians were told about the diversities of Spiritual gifts and the fact that although there were diversities, the gifts came from the same Spirit. God has not called us to be clones or robots, but to be unique in the Holy Spirit. Each individual in the body of Christ whom He has gifted is unique, and we must not resist and reject the gift because of the uniqueness of the person prophesying; let's not get caught up in the personality but in the Spirit. This is why it is imperative that we have the discerning of spirits because someone's flow in the Holy Ghost may be different from what we are accustomed to and this can cause us to shun that person and miss what the Holy Ghost is doing. There are some congregations that are so controlled that the expression of prophecy and other gifts are stifled because of the diverse ways in which they manifest. I am not advocating a free for all in our services, but I do believe the Spirit of the Lord manifests in different ways and if we are sensitive to His leading we should embrace His diverse mode of operation and manifestation.

The Corinthians were told by Paul that there are differences of administrations and diversities of operations of the gifts, but they all are from the same Lord; The manifestation, administration and operation may differ but the source never changes. *"But the manifestation of the Spirit is given to every man to profit withal" (2 Corinthians 12:7).* We must resist the temptation to believe only the individuals with a title before their names, or a certain level of theological education, is gifted. If you are a child of Christ who is filled with His Holy Spirit, you have been endued with a Spiritual gift or gifts and God wants the gift or gifts to manifest and be in operation for His glory. Maybe you never got hooked

on phonics or you only speak Ebonics; if you belong to Christ, God has gifted you and you should not allow your shortcomings to stifle or impede the gift. By all means you should strive to educate yourself, but never allow low self esteem or a spirit of intimidation to hinder you from going forth in your gift. When Paul said the manifestation is given to every man that is what he meant; since he went on to say there is neither male nor female in Christ, man can be used generically to mean mankind which includes sisters also. In *1 Corinthians 12:8-10* he listed the gifts given by the Spirit:

1) The word of *wisdom*
2) The word of *knowledge*
3) The gift of *faith*
4) The gifts of *healing*
5) The working of miracles
6) The gift of prophecy
7) The gift of discerning of spirits
8) The gift of divers kinds of tongues
9) The gift of interpretation of tongues

According to the apostle, all nine gifts work through the Spirit, and he divides to every person severally as He will. If you are filled with the Spirit of God, then at least one or more of the aforementioned gifts should be in operation. Some will dare to say miracles have ceased, some will say tongues have ceased and some would dare to say prophesy has ceased; my question to these people is this: has the Spirit ceased, and have the saints been perfected, edified and come to the measure and the stature of a perfect man? The answer is absolutely not. Listen to what Paul told the Corinthians: *"If any man thinks himself to be a prophet, or spiritual, let him acknowledge that the things that I write unto you are the commandments of the Lord. Wherefore, brethren, covet to prophesy, and forbid not to speak with tongues"* (1 Corinthians 14:37, 39).

Stir up the Gift

Paul told his spiritual son Timothy not to neglect the gift that was in him-the gift that was given to him by prophecy, through the laying on of hands of the presbytery. Timothy was instructed by Paul to,"meditate on those things and to give himself wholly to them and his profiting would appear to all." We do not have to jockey for position in the body of Christ, neither do we have to look for men to validate us. Through the Holy Spirit, we have a gift on the inside; we should stir it up and the manifestation will be visible to all for the glory of God.

The final book of our Bible, the book of Revelation is a prophetic book. It is a prophetic revelation of Jesus Christ given to the Church by God of things that must come to pass. It can be a very challenging book because of the series of apocalyptic revelations received by John, but verse 3 states, *"Blessed is he that readeth, and they that hear the words of this prophecy, and keep those things which are written therein: for the time is at hand.* Beloved, embrace the Spirit of prophecy and God will reveal things to you which are about to come to past.

Edification

Fidel Donaldson

Paul gave the Corinthian Church three components to New Testament prophecy and I believe these three components should accompany prophecy today. The prophetic word comes from God to man, and according to Paul, it is for edification. The Greek word for edification is oikodome and it means architecture, a structure or a building; it is a compound of the words oikos and doma. Oikos refers to a dwelling, a home or a temple. The word doma means to build; an edifice, specially a roof or housetop.

The Apostle used the same word in his letter to the Ephesians in describing the purpose of the five-fold ministry gifts given to the church by the Lord Jesus. The prophets along with the apostle, the evangelist, the pastor and the teacher are responsible for edifying the body of Christ. Their responsibility is to build the body to a place where it becomes a temple or dwelling place for the presence of God.

The true prophet of God does not keep the people dependent on the prophetic word coming from his or her mouth like a baby dependent on her mother's milk, but builds them through Biblically sound prophetic teaching to hear and speak the word on their own. We must be careful not to become so mesmerized with the prophet or the prophetic gift that we ignore the fact that there should be a word that builds, exhorts, and comforts when God sends His prophet into our midst. There has been a proliferation of the prophetic over the years and that is a good thing, because the Bible states that as one of the things that will be evident in the last days. We have to be cognizant of the fact that where the genuine is manifested, the counterfeit will try to masquerade itself. The gift of discerning of Spirits will help us to identify the true prophet from the false. It is important that we do not allow emotions to cloud our judgment and our discernment. When a word is coming forth, we have to make sure it is a word coming from God through the mouth of a true prophet, failure to do so can cause great harm.

A Prophet Dies for Disobedience

In *1 Samuel Chapter 13*, we get an illustration of this from an encounter between a young prophet and an old prophet. The young prophet was sent by God to deliver a word and was instructed by God not to eat bread nor drink water and not to travel back the same way that he came. On his way home, he met an old prophet who invited him to eat bread. He explained to the old prophet that God had instructed him not to eat bread or drink water in that place. Listen to what the old prophet said to him, *"I am a prophet also as thou art; and an angel spake unto me by the word of the LORD, saying, Bring him back with thee into thine house, that he may eat bread and drink water. But he lied to him."* The young prophet fell for the lie and went back to his house and ate bread and drank water. As they were eating and drinking, the word of the LORD came to the old prophet informing the young prophet that, *"his carcass would not come unto the sepulcher of his fathers,"* in other words he was going to die for his disobedience.

Obedience is better than sacrifice and disobedience can lead to death. When God gives us instructions, it is very important that we obey Him, no matter who says other wise. Paul told the Galatians, *"But though we, or an angel from heaven, preach any other gospel unto you than that which we have preached unto you, let him be accursed (Galatians 1:8).* If you don't have discernment, you better get caller ID because you need to know who is speaking.

Personal Testimony

I can recall the time when I planned to take a trip to England to smuggle drugs and could not find my passport. My wife spoke to me and told me that God did not want me to take that trip and warned me that if I went, there would be problems. I told her off and practically tore the house apart to find it. When I did, I held it up to her and told her that God wanted me to go because if He didn't, I would not have found the passport. I was very deceived at that time. I made it to England, but was in prison by the next day, and wound up serving three years out of an eight year prison sentence. Warning truly comes before destruction and a haughty spirit before a fall.

Exhortation

The other purpose for New Testament prophecy is *exhortation.* The Greek word for exhortation is *paraklesis* which comes from the word Parakaleo and it means, *to call near, to invite, to comfort, to pray or to intreat.* The prophetic voice calls, invites and exhorts us in to the presence of the Lord. In Romans 12:1, when Paul beseeches us by the mercies of God to present our bodies a living sacrifice, the same word *Parakaleo* is used. The prophetic word should never drive us away from God, but it should challenge us to get to a place where we can dwell in God's presence. In *Luke 10,* in the story of the prodigal son, we see the father entreating the angry, older brother to enter the house where the fatted calf was killed, music was playing and dancing was taking place to celebrate the return of the younger son.

Comfort

The third word Paul used for the purpose of prophecy is the word *comfort* which comes from the Greek word *paramutheomai* (pronounced par-am-oo-thee'-ah); *It* means *to relate near, encourage, console.* This definition is interesting when you consider the fact that the Holy Ghost is called the comforter and He plays an integral part in prophecy and in getting us into the presence of the Lord; as a matter of fact, He is the key to all components to prophecy. Jesus Christ is edifying or building us as His church through the power of the Holy Spirit. It is the Holy Spirit who invites, exhorts and entreats us to draw near to God. As well as the one who comforts us.

Personal Testimony

I am baffled by the fact there are some in the body of Christ who believe prophecy is not for today. The prophet is one of the five ministry gifts given to the church by the Lord Jesus Christ for the perfecting of the saints, for the work of the ministry, for edifying of the body of Christ: till we all come in the unity of the faith, and of the knowledge of the Son of God, unto a perfect man, unto the measure of the stature of the fullness of Christ *(Ephesians 4:12-13).* With this awareness, I have to ask some questions: Have the saints been perfected? Has the body of Christ reached full edification? Are we all unified in faith and in the knowledge of the Son of God? Have we reached the measure of the stature of the fullness of Christ? The answer is evidently an emphatic no! Would anyone in his or her right mind say the ministry of the evangelist, pastor, and teacher has ceased. If those three are still active and Jesus gave five, why then do some people say the ministry of the prophet is not for today?

Personal Encounter with the Prophetic

Years ago when I came home from England where I received salvation, my sister took me to visit a church on Merrick Boulevard, in Jamaica Queens called, *Beginning a New Life Worship Center.* The church was led by a dynamic and charismatic man of God by the name of Andre Cook; we called him Prophet Cook because flowed heavily in the prophetic anointing and he loved praise, worship, and prayer. The worship was led by an awesome and anointed young man by the name Michael Pugh. My wife and I became faith partners of the ministry because our home church was Mount Olivet Gospel Church, in Corona Queens.

In that small assembly I witnessed first hand the power of worship, the moving of the Spirit and the prophetic. I received quite a few prophecies from the man of God in New York, but it was not until I relocated to Jacksonville, Florida and invited him to speak at a conference I convened in the month of March that he spoke a life transforming word over my wife and me. As a preface to the prophecy, I need to tell you that my wife and I along with our children had some great financial struggles when we lived in New York, largely because of the carnal lifestyle that landed me in prison in England. One of the things I prayed for was to own a home, so my children could have a place to call home. There was nothing in the natural that was conducive to home ownership because our credit was messed up, and as Apostle Jerald I Perry would say, *"our money looked funny and our change looked strange."* I tell the story of how we were so poor the rats and the roaches moved to another house so they wouldn't starve to death. One day my son looked at me with a bewildered look on his face and said, *"Daddy we are poor;"* It didn't take much discernment to figure that one out. In those desperate times I did my best to stay faithful in the things of God; I kept worshipping God and was voracious in my appetite for the word.

When I planned the conference, one of the members of the church I attended in Jacksonville took the time to drive me around to hand out flyers to promote the conference; I asked the Lord to bless her for her faithfulness. When Prophet Cook was receiving the offering, she was the first one out of her seat with a check. As soon as she put it in his hands, he told her that the Lord would move for her in three months. It is interesting to note that the conference took place in March, the third month, and he told her God would move for her in three months. The number three in the Bible represents resurrection, completion and perfection. After receiving the offering for the evening, he called my wife and me to him and told us prophetically that before the year was out we would be in our own home with little or no money down. As previously stated, there was nothing in the natural conducive to homeownership, but I knew it was a bona fide word from the mouth of the Prophet of God, so I tucked it away in my heart. One night we were in service, and the young lady who received the prophetic word from Prophet Cook came forward to give a testimony.

She told the congregation that she received a call about some law suit money that was held up, the person on the call informed her that a check was being sent to her in the amount of $80,000; that event took place in June and my mind immediately went back to the word she received in March that God would move for her in three months. At that point my mind began to be focused on the word the prophet had given my wife and me that night. Three months had gone by, and we had not so much as looked at a house; we had faith in the prophetic word, but faith without works is dead. God will make provision for the house, but He is not going to do the house hunting or the leg work for us. Has God spoken to you about something that your finances or your credit cannot produce? Trust him and do the leg work necessary to manifest the substance and evidence you hope for.

Not long after she gave the testimony, the young lady called my wife and me and told us about a realtor whom she knew. We made an appointment with the gentleman. I told him from the outset that it would be God doing it because we did not have the finances or the credit to get it done. I mentioned to him that my wife had a couple of student loans, so he went on line to check it out. In New York City, there were business schools that popped up all over and some of them had nefarious motives. They enticed prospective students to take out loans to be enrolled, but on many occasions teachers never showed up and at the end of the day, the student was stuck with the responsibility of repaying the loan which went on their credit if they defaulted.

When he looked up my wife's loan, he realized that the bank that held the note was indicted for fraud and one of the managers actually went to prison. With that information I wrote the credit bureaus and presented that information and my wife's credit score went up. God is not going to allow the prophetic word spoken to us through the mouth of his servant the prophet to fall to the ground. When God is ready to activate that word, He will expose corruption in high places and do whatever else is necessary to bring His word to fruition.

We started looking for a house although we did not have much finances, but we were armed with a prophetic word from the Lord that said, *"Before the year was out we would be in our own home with little or no money down."* The prophet had told my wife that when she saw the house she would know it. I saw some houses that I thought were the one, but my wife did not feel the release. I looked at the houses with the people's furniture in it, but my wife looked at them from another perspective. She pictured the house with her furniture, so in her mind she took note of the closet space and the size of the bedrooms. By the end of October, I was feeling some pressure because I had testified to friends and family that God was going to provide a house for us before the year was out, well the year was coming to a close, and a spirit of doubt tried to attach itself to me, but

Fidel Donaldson

I shook it off and kept praising God. One day the realtor took us into a certain neighborhood and showed us a nice four bedroom house. My wife felt the witness that it was the house! Years before, I prayed that each of our children would have their own room and four bedrooms would allow each of our three children to have their own room.

Moving on up Like George and Weezie

When God says the end of the year, He means the end of the year. Whenever I think of this testimony, it makes me rejoice. In *March 2002*, Prophet Andre Cook prophesied we would be in our own home before the year was out; On *December 31st, 2002*, the last day of the last month of the year my wife and I were in a closing agents office signing papers and receiving the keys to our new home; we packed our Dodge Caravan and began to move up like George and Weezie Jefferson. Our God is the God of 11:59 and 59 in that if He tells you prophetically that something is going to happen before the year is out, stand on the word and do not panic because heaven and earth will pass away before His word returns to Him void! God's prophetic word in your life will come to pass no matter how much time has passed. Don't allow the elapse of time to cause you to panic and give way to fear and doubt. Worship Him and let the prophetic voice flow out of you so things can manifest.

The enemy loves when we doubt God because the manifestation has not come. God is sovereign and all powerful and nothing can stop

Praise Worship and the Spirit of Prophecy

His word from coming to pass. Fear and doubt can cause us to toss and turn, but if God has spoken it, it must come to pass; Hallelujah!

We are in tough economic times right now and many people are losing their homes due to foreclosure, but thanks be to God that despite layoffs and the loss of businesses, we are still residing in the home God provided prophetically many years ago because we believed his prophet. Beloved, *"believe His prophets so shall you prosper"* (2 *Chronicles 20:20).* When you have that type of testimony such as my wife and I have, why would we believe for a moment that the ministry of the prophet and prophecy is not for today?

Tassel's Testimony

I had the privilege of ministering for The Prayer Squad in Margate Florida recently. On Saturday morning I called my friend Dr. Tassel Daley to see how she was doing. I was in total amazement during our conversation when Dr. T as she is affectionately known began to talk about worship and the spirit of prophecy; she was unaware of the fact the Lord had me sequestered up to eight hours a day typing this manuscript. I knew right away she was speaking to me through the unction of the Holy Spirit. After informing her I was writing on the same topic, I told her that my wife and I were on our way to see her. When we arrived I explained to her about the book I was working on and the awesome confirmation that came from her. I felt an urgency to ask her to proofread the material and thank God she agreed. I have called her several times to see how the proof reading was coming along and she shared with me on the phone some of the things she was gleaning from the book.

This morning when I arose and checked my phone, I noticed several missed calls from Dr. T and called her immediately. From the time I placed the manuscript in her hands, I had a sense that as she read it, the Spirit of the Lord would lead her into a deep place of worship and prophecy. When she answered the phone, she said she was trying to reach me to share a testimony. I was very excited about hearing it. She told me she was reading the testimony about the prophetic word my wife and I received which led to home ownership, and she had to pause for a worship break because the Spirit of the Lord was moving. While she was worshipping, she received a call from her brother and his wife informing her that they had to speak with her, so she went to their place immediately. Her brother, his wife and their children live at the same complex as Dr. T; as a matter of fact, he and his wife own the Condo where Dr. T resides. When she arrived at their place, they informed her that they were blessing her with the condo. What a mighty God we serve. The condo is free and clear, meaning there is no mortgage attached to the property. When the Lord spoke to her brother through the Holy Spirit to bless her with the condo, he wondered how his wife would react. Unbeknownst to him, the Holy

Spirit had spoken and confirmed the same thing to his wife because there is power in agreement. What an awesome testimony! In the

Praise Worship and the Spirit of Prophecy

midst of Dr. T's worship, the Spirit of the Lord moved on the man and woman of God and they were obedient.

Whatever you stand in need of at the present time, take a moment now and set an atmosphere of worship that is conducive to the moving of the Holy Spirit. What the Lord did for Dr. T He can do for you because our Father in heaven is no respecter of persons. It does not matter what type of environment you are in as you read this. It could be a maximum or minimum security prison, it could be the bed of affliction in a hospital or a convalescent home, or it could be at a place where you are battling depression because of some great loss. Worship will cause a transformation of the atmosphere and cause miracles to break forth. Worship God and prophesy by the power of the Holy Ghost in the name of Jesus.

I had spoken to Dr. T about being on radio and TV because of the wealth of knowledge and the anointing of God upon her life. I told her what she has on the inside cannot be kept to herself. When her brother and his wife gave her the wonderful news that she was now the owner of the free and clear condo, they also told her that His wife's mother was opening a door for her to be a regular guest on a television program in the Cayman Islands. Beloved, worship facilitates the prophetic voice in us, so when we worship, we should expect a move of God to take place. Expectation is the birthing ground of miracles.

Fidel Donaldson

PART FIVE

Praise Worship and the Spirit of Prophecy

CHAPTER 13

There Is a Prophetic Word in Your Belly

As children of God, we should not underestimate the power of God's word that dwells in us through study and meditation. The Apostle Paul said the word of God is so near to us that it is in our mouth and in our heart; he called it the word of faith. Faith demonstrates to the eye of the mind that which is not readily seen by the eye of the body; faith is a firm expectation and persuasion that God will do exactly what He promised. We must not allow the negative things we see and hear to hinder us from speaking the prophetic word of faith. Sometimes we have a tendency to doubt ourselves because of the things we lack or because of our human frailties, but we should always remember the words of Paul when he declared, *"we have this treasure in earthen vessels that the excellency and the power may be of God and not of ourselves"* (*2 Corinthians 4:7*) God has chosen us as His vessels for a dwelling place of His Spirit and His Word. Great men of God in the Bible were apprehensive when called upon by God to speak His word but God would not have any of their excuses.

Praise Worship and the Spirit of Prophecy

Jeremiah was a descendant from a line of priests from Anathoth in the land of Benjamin, but he was ordained by God to be a prophet. It is important to note that it was God who ordained Jeremiah and not man. In speaking to His disciples Jesus declared, *"Ye have not chosen me, but I have chosen you, and ordained you, that ye should go and bring forth fruit, and that your fruit should remain: that whatsoever ye shall ask of the Father in my name, he may give it you" (John 15:16).*

I know some of us like to have these elaborate ordination services with a great deal of pomp and pageantry and that is ok, but I want to let you know that God has chosen you and ordained you to be a prophetic fruit producer in the earth, so don't hold back because man has not laid hands on you or has not released you. Man's ordination has the glitz and the glamour, but God's ordination has fruit, and it has the fruit that remains. Please do not get me wrong; I am not against services to set someone apart in the congregation for service to the Lord, I just want to establish the fact that man can only affirm what God has already confirmed; The power and the authority that man has, is given to him by God, so we must always remember that the gift is given by God then confirmed by the presbytery. There are some individuals who have sat around for years with gifts in them and they have not gone forth in that particular gift because they don't have a title bestowed or have not been released. I believe in order and decency, but when we stand before God to give an account of how we invested His talent(s) we will not be able to say," the apostle the bishop or the pastor did not release me." Do not sit around frustrated, get yourself in a church that believes in training, equipping and sending out, so you can do what God has called, sanctified and ordained you to do.

The word of the LORD came to Jeremiah informing him that God knew him before he formed him in the belly, sanctified him before he came out of the womb and ordained him a prophet to the nations. What an awesome call! Jeremiah is not the only prophet in the Bible to receive a touch from God in the womb. John the Baptist' mother Elizabeth was filled with the Holy Ghost and John began to leap in the womb. Can you imagine being ordained a prophet to the nations before you come out of the womb? You may be called to minister prophetically to a few, and that is ok because the same God who consecrated and ordained Jeremiah a prophet to the nations is the same God who sanctified and called you.

Don't allow your Disability to affect your Availability

When he received the word from God, he adopted a posture like Moses, in that; he wanted to back out of the call by presenting his disability to God. He told the LORD that he could not speak because he was a child. God will not allow us to use any disability as an excuse because He is not looking for ability but availability; whatever we lack in fulfilling our calling and assignment, He will equip us with the necessary tools to get the job done; As a matter of fact, once the Holy Spirit is on the inside of us we are already equipped with everything we need. Listen to the words of Jesus concerning the kingdom of God: *"And when he was demanded of the Pharisees, when the kingdom of God should come, he answered them said, The kingdom of God cometh not with observation: Neither shall they say, Lo here! Or, lo there! For, behold, the kingdom of God is within you"* (*Luke 17:20-21*). There are things we are seeking through external sources and the key to unlocking those things are on the inside of us; through the Spirit and the Word we have access to the kingdom of God who calls those things that be not as though they already are. John declared, *"greater is he that is in you, than he that is in the world"* (*1 John 4:4*).

Irrespective of how we feel or how bad things appear to be, the greater one is on the inside so we should believe and act upon what He has spoken and not what the world has spoken.

Has God put a prophetic word in your belly? Yes He has. Have you allowed feelings of inadequacy, spiritual low self esteem, or fear to cripple you? Pray and ask God the Holy Spirit to fill you with boldness so you can speak as His oracle. I know there are times when we may feel apprehensive about speaking because we may not be sure it is a word from the LORD, but we cannot allow apprehension and fear to quench the Spirit and stop the prophetic word from flowing. Fear and doubt will put us in bondage and that is why we need to move in the power of the Spirit. The Spirit of the Lord gives us the liberty to flow in the things of God, *"Now the Lord is that Spirit: and where the Spirit of the Lord is, there is liberty"* (*2 Corinthians 3:17*).

At one point Jeremiah told God he would not speak or make mention of God's name because of the persecution he came under, but God refused to let him off the hook, instead God turned up the heat until the prophetic word felt like *"fire shut up in his bones."* I have been in services where I witnessed someone holding their belly as if it was on fire, I wonder if they were having a *'fire shut up in the bones moment'*

God told Jeremiah he would go where he sent him and speak whatever he commanded him to speak, and he should not be afraid of the people's faces because God would be with him to deliver the word. The LORD put His words in Jeremiah's mouth and that day set him over the nations, kingdoms, to root out, and to pull down, and to destroy, and to throw down, to build, and to plant.

Our calling and our assignment may not be as dramatic, but when God saved us and we received the gift of the Holy Spirit, He put a word in our belly and we must be bold when it is time to speak that word. There are times when God has spoken to me and instead of speaking I kept silent for whatever reason, and the next thing I knew, someone else came forward and spoke the very thing God had spoken to me. The enemy will use various tactics and devices to hinder the prophetic in our belly from coming forth, but we must not be ignorant of his devices and we should be ready to bring forth the prophetic word with boldness as the Spirit gives us utterance.

Dancing in the Rain

Several years ago when I lived in Queens, New York, I attend a community event in East *Elmhurst Queens at PS 127*. Once a year, the people of the community would come together and fellowship. It was a great opportunity to see people I had not seen in a long time. There

Praise Worship and the Spirit of Prophecy

was vendor space available for people who wanted to sell things and since I had a clothing business at the time, I rented a space. I had my wife, our children, her sister Sylvia, and her aunt Iona who is a devout praying woman, present at the location that day. I set up my table and was prepared to put out the apparel, when I noticed a few rain drops had come down on the pristine white table cloth I had spread. A down pour would have put a damper on the event and definitely would have wrecked any hope I had of making some sales.

I remember looking up towards the heavens and declaring that there would be no rain while we were out there for the festivities. I learned the power of the spoken word that day when the rain did not fall. The sun was shining brightly and people were strolling leisurely up and down the street having a good time. After awhile, I felt a few drops of rain again and I kept making the declaration. I vividly remember an evangelist from *Mount Olivet Gospel Church* where we attended, who stopped to converse with us; and while we were talking she mentioned the possibility of it raining to which I responded immediately that it would not rain. I kept releasing the word into the atmosphere that God was going to hold up the rain.

Lord send the Rain

We spent hours outdoors having a good time; I remember as the sunshine began to give way to evening and evening began to turn to night we started to pack away the clothes. What I experienced next was an incredible manifestation of the power of the word spoken in faith, and the ability by faith to decree and declare something and see it come to pass. It was so incredible that I rarely speak about it and have never written about it before. When everything was packed away in the car, I looked up to the heavens and said: *"Send it down now Lord."* As soon as I finished speaking, there was lightning and thunder followed by a torrential down pour of rain. The adults around me knew what was taking place because they heard me in the beginning when I prayed for the rain to be held up and declared it would not rain while we had our things out there. At the end of the event, they heard me calling the rain down. Aunty Iona was the first one to dance in the rain as she praised God for the miracle she witnessed. It didn't take long for the rest of us, including the children, to join in with the praises and the dancing. I know the people who were scurrying for shelter may have thought that we lost it, but we didn't care what people thought; we had just witnessed a mighty move of God and all we wanted to do was glorify His name.

People may think it was a coincidence or some may doubt whether or not it ever happened but I call it a God-incident. I've been teased by people all my life when they become aware that my name is Fidel due to the reputation Fidel Castro has in certain places. But Fidel means faith and my faith was strengthened and solidified that day as I experienced something that can never be taken away from me. Kathryn Kuhlman said, *"I believe in miracles because I believe in God"* and I strongly concur. The Spirit of God on the inside of us and the word of God in us will facilitate signs, wonders and miracles.

Praise Worship and the Spirit of Prophecy

The Prophetic Prayer Room

There is a room in the back of my home that is set apart for prayer, praise and worship. Every Thursday evening when my schedule permits, the SWAT TEAM gathers there for intense and profuse worship and prayer with an expectation of a prophetic flow, and God never disappoints. We have experienced a plethora of testimonies of a manifestation of the prophetic word directly attributable to the intense atmosphere of worship. Please allow me to share one with you.

The Prophet from Mesquite

One evening, I was in the room with some worship music playing while I waited for the rest of the team to arrive. While I was there in worship I felt the unction of the Holy Spirit to go to my bedroom. When I entered the room, my wife was talking on the phone and she had our cell phone bill in her hand. I could surmise from her side of the conversation that she had some questions about some of the charges on the bill. The Holy Spirit spoke to me and told me to go back to the room and get back in worship. I had my cell phone on the podium on vibrate and as I was in the room worshipping I could see the light on my phone flashing. When I answered the phone, I recognized the voice on the other end to be that of my dear friend and brother in the Lord, Prophet Emmanuel Haniah, a man of God anointed to prophesy. With a strong emphatic voice he yelled, *"Man of God how much is your cell phone bill this month?"* I was in awe of the timing of the Holy Ghost speaking through his prophet, and knew immediately that it was not a coincidence. I had just come from the bedroom and witnessed my wife dealing with the issue with the cell phone company, and in minutes God had His servant calling from Mesquite Texas to pay the bill. He had no clue my wife was on the phone discussing the bill and neither did I until I went to the room, but our omniscient God knew.

When I inquired as to why he called at that particular moment to inquire about my cell phone bill of all things, he said he was driving his son home from school and the Holy Spirit spoke to him so he pulled over. When he did, his son asked him why he was pulling over to which he informed him that the Holy Spirit told him to pay my cell phone bill.

God knows every need we have and He is able to supply all our needs according to His riches in glory by Christ Jesus. The riches are in the glory and worship is the vehicle that transports us from the earth realm into the glory realm; worship either transports us or it brings the glory to our realm. Everything we need is in the glory. If we stay in that posture of Spirit led worship, we will tap into the glory, and God will supply the need in a timely manner.

In the same manner which Jehoshaphat and the children of Judah worshipped before going into battle and worshipped when they received the victory, we must start our activities with worship and end them in worship. There have been a proliferation of prayer phone lines over the years, and I have noticed on some of them that the people go right into prayer without praise, worship and welcoming the presence of the Holy Spirit. How can we come before God to make our petitions

Praise Worship and the Spirit of Prophecy

known without first setting the atmosphere in worship? I would go as far as to say that some of the things we pray about will manifest if we set an atmosphere of worship that can produce a prophetic word. We need the Spirit to help our infirmities when we pray, and worship takes us beyond ourselves and magnifies God.

Fidel Donaldson

CHAPTER 14

It's Time to Prophesy

Prior to reading this book, you may have thought you were not qualified to prophecy; you may have had doubts about New Testament prophecy because of the excesses of certain individuals who call themselves prophets. The fact that there has been a proliferation of prophets over the years should not come as a surprise to anyone; once again, remember what Peter said on the day of Pentecost when he quoted the prophet Joel? He said God would pour out His Spirit in the last days and sons, daughters, servants and handmaidens would prophesy. There is no question we are in the last days, because of the darkness that is increasing in the earth and in people. Most Christians know we are in the last days and one of the signs will be an outpouring of God's Spirit that will facilitate the proliferation of the prophetic.

I believe each individual has a great part to play in the sphere in which he or she operates. I also believe that the sphere in which we live is in large part affected or shaped by our thoughts, our speech, and our actions. The words that we speak, whether positive or negative can greatly influence our atmosphere. As Christians, we read

Praise Worship and the Spirit of Prophecy

scriptures, hear preaching and teaching, and sing songs about the greatness of our God, but some of us when faced with a need, instead of prophesying of an increase through the Spirit, we speak the negativity of the situation.

The spoken word is a very powerful thing that can shift the atmosphere and bring transformation for better or for worse. To understand the power of the spoken word we need look no further than the creation and the fact that God spoke it into being. There will be times when we may feel overwhelmed by the sheer magnitude of the situation we are facing, but we should not allow any situation to have us in a state of mind where we resign ourselves to the situation and speak doubt instead of victory. Condition the mind to speak prophetic words of life. Habits are easy to form but hard to break. Mind transformation does not take place overnight especially if our thoughts have been negative over a long period of time. Our minds must be renewed through the Spirit in order for our prophetic utterances to line up with the Word of God. Many of us have encountered people who never seem to have anything positive to say. Association brings assimilation so we must be careful not to allow the spirit of pessimism to attach itself to us. Job asked God to, *"Teach me, and I will hold my tongue: and cause me to understand wherein I have erred" (Job 6:24).* When faced with a situation that is negative, we should not speak in haste but wait for the Spirit to give us the words to speak. My dad expressed to me that his dad informed him that you cannot take back a spoken word or a spent coin. Once we release the word, it is in the atmosphere for better or for worse, so it is advisable that we think before we speak. In the instances where we have allowed negative confessions to cause blight in the atmosphere, all we need to do is repent and speak positively instead. As Dr. Tassel noted,"God has given us the power to reverse the curse of negative words. Through ignorance we might have spoken negative words but praise God we have the God-given power and opportunity to reverse it by rebuking the negative words spoken and replacing them with positive ones."

The Power of the Tongue

"*Death and life are in the power of the tongue: and they that love it shall eat the fruit thereof*" *(Proverbs 1:21).* I am amazed at the amount of negativity I hear coming out of the mouths of so many people, especially some Christians. I constantly have to tell people to speak the solution and not the problem. I've held conferences in other cities and invited people to go with me and the first word out of their mouths is, "*I don't have any money.*" The statement may be true but why should it be the first words articulated when, "*God gives seed to the sower.*" When we have something to do and it pertains to the Kingdom of God, and the finances are not available, we must take God's word to Him and let Him know that we need seed to sow into the kingdom project. Once we open our mouths and release a word about what we can't do, that word creates a negative atmosphere which helps to maintain the status quo; if the status quo is lack in a certain area, we certainly do not want to continue it through the words we speak. Satan is the Prince of the power of the air and his minions will use those words against us.

The Bible records an incident when Jesus was traveling with His disciples and saw a fig tree with leaves from afar, but when He approached the tree Jesus noticed that there were no figs on it only leaves. Jesus spoke these words to the tree, *"Let no fruit grow on thee henceforward for ever" (Matthew 21:19).* Things can look fruitful from a distance, but upon closer inspection you see the lack of fruitfulness. When the disciples saw the withered fig tree, they marveled at how quickly it withered away. Jesus told them if they have faith and do not doubt they could do the same thing to the fig tree, and speak to a mountain and tell it to be removed into the sea.

According to what Jesus told them, the disciples have the word in their mouths to curse things that are not bearing fruit and to cause mountains that are in their way to be removed and this is done through the power of the tongue; with that being said it is important to note that our words must be backed up by faith. Are we stifling and stagnating our own blessings when we constantly use the words 'I can't or I don't?' Since God is the one who gives the seed to the sower and the bread to the eater, we should speak to Him when we need seed to sow and bread to eat.

Prophetic or Pathetic

When faced with circumstances that we have not the wherewithal to deal with, will the words coming out of our mouths be Prophetic or Pathetic? In *Hebrews 11:3*, the Bible tells us that God formed the worlds in which we live through the word that He spoke so that things which are seen were not made by things which do appear. The raw materials used by man to make things were given to him by Almighty God who dwells in an unseen realm. God sent the Word to tabernacle among men and now we have the Word and the Spirit living on the inside of us. We can use that same word now to call those things that be not as though they already were. At a certain point in creation, the world that God framed was without form, it was void, and it was covered by darkness. God did not panic because of the formless void dark earth; the Spirit of God moved on the face of the waters and God spoke and light appeared. When we are faced with a void dark situation, let's not panic and resign ourselves to it. The Spirit and the Word work together to fulfill the purpose and plan of God, so speak the word and cause light to appear.

Manifestation in the Prayer Room

One night the prayer team and I were in the prayer room in worship, and one of the team members, Prophetess Waltina Bellamy began to speak prophetically about seeing some zeros. She kept saying she did not know whether or not it was 500 or a 1,000 but she kept seeing them. In the midst of intense worship, God will show us things. At some point she turned to me and told me that I was about to get a 'suddenly,' As soon as I heard that, I began to get deeper in worship because I needed a 'suddenly'. Early the next morning my door bell rang and I went to answer it. When I opened the door a friend stepped in and put a check in my hand and told me he kept

Praise Worship and the Spirit of Prophecy

telling God five hundred, but God said no a thousand. When I looked at the check, it was for $1,000.00 dollars. I was amazed because he was not in the prayer room the night before and had no idea about the word Prophetess Bellamy received while we were in worship. I am thoroughly convinced that what he did was a direct result of the prophetic atmosphere we created in worship. The fact that he halted between two amounts like Sister Bellamy did was further confirmation that both of them heard from God at some point; when I received the $1,000.00 check, I surely was overjoyed at the fact that God gave him the correct amount which was the larger amount.

I am not advocating we frivolously throw words around: 'in a name it and claim, blab it and grab it fashion,' but what I am suggesting is that we train our minds to speak and prophesy the word of God. We should not be so quick to speak about what we don't have or what we cannot do, but we should endeavor, like children who know they have a heavenly Father who is Omnipotent, Omniscient, and Omnipresent, to speak like we trust Him and know beyond a shadow of a doubt that He is working on our behalf. Glory!

As previously stated, we should not underestimate the power of the spoken word and its ability to produce life or to produce death. When Jesus came to Capernaum, a centurion came to Him for healing for his servant who was sick and grievously tormented. Jesus agreed to go to his home and heal his servant, but before they left, the centurion said something that caused Jesus to marvel. He told Jesus that he was not worthy for Him to come under his roof; but Jesus should, *"speak the word only, and my servant shall be healed"* (*Matthew 8:8*). Jesus marveled because he had not found great faith like the centurion had in Israel. The centurion was a Roman soldier and not of the nation of Israel, but he understood authority and the power of the spoken word. He understood the type of authority Jesus walked in and knew that His authority was not limited to Him being at the location for the healing to take place. He knew that a healing word from the mouth of Jesus would suffice. *"He sent his word, and healed them, and delivered them from their destructions" (Psalm 107:20).* The word of faith in our mouth is not limited, it is unlimited. The only thing that can hinder it is the spirit of fear.

Whatever the condition you are dealing with, there is a commensurate word to bring healing and deliverance, but that word must flow from a heart and mind of faith. The mouth speaks from the abundance of the heart, so if the heart is filled with fear and doubt, the mouth will speak accordingly and that is why we must fill our hearts and minds with the word of God, and be willing to speak that word with faith.

A Healing Word

One night, I was invited to do some teaching on a prayer line and I was teaching on the importance of being on one accord and how that posture of unity brought a 'suddenly' for the one hundred and twenty disciples in the upper room, and for Paul and Silas when they were in the Philippian Jail. Prior to getting on the line, I had an excruciating headache and lower back pain that were causing some painful spasms

Praise Worship and the Spirit of Prophecy

in my leg. When I logged into the line, I heard the saints praying, so I put my hand on my head and prayed with them. After the teaching I instructed the individuals on the line to praise God and believe Him for a 'suddenly.' There was a loud chorus of praise coming through the line and I joined in and began to fill the house with praise; while I was praising I asked God for a suddenly in my body and I can tell you truthfully that the pain in my head, my lower back and my leg lifted and I received the healing by faith that I spoke over my body. God has placed His Spirit and His Word in us, so we can speak boldly and cause things to shift and to be transformed. There are times we are waiting on God to speak, and He is waiting on us. The Prophet Elijah told King Ahab, *"As the LORD God of Israel liveth, before whom I stand, there shall not be dew nor rain these years, but according to my word"* (1 Kings 17:1). Before he spoke the word he told King Ahab that he stood before God, signifying the fact that he was speaking as God's ambassador and that is why he was able to say, *"according to my word."*

God is not a respecter of persons and does not love us any less than he loved Elijah or any of the prophets; the difference is in the level of obedience. Men like Elijah and women like Deborah took God at His word and were willing to speak that word with boldness. Are you down to your last at the present time? Does your situation seem hopeless? Speak the word, prophesy to that mountain or curse the infirmity sickness and disease that is blocking your future and causing you to be unproductive. Has the judge handed you a lengthy sentence that does not reflect the crime? Do not settle, even though the odds appear to be against you. Continue to bombard the atmosphere with faith backed prophetic words of deliverance. I spoke earlier about the recording of Ella Fitzgerald's voice having the ability to shatter a glass and the shout of the Israelites bringing down the walls encompassing Jericho. There is an octave, a pitch and a sound in the voice of every child of God that causes such a ripple and vibration that it can tear down walls and caused things that hold us back to be shattered.

When the king of Syria sent a letter to the king of Israel about healing Naaman the leper, the king of his Israel was gripped by fear and rent his clothes. When the Prophet Elisha heard that the king of Israel rent his clothes, he sent to the king saying, *"Wherefore hast thou rent thy clothes? Let him come now to me, and he shall know that there is a prophet in Israel" (2 Kings 5:8).* We should not be cocky but we should definitely be confident in the word God has placed in our mouths. Like his father in the Lord Elijah, the Prophet Elisha knew that he was God's representative, and that he had the power to speak to Naaman's leprosy. We must be confident in the word God has invested in us, and we must show that confidence by not shrinking into despair due to the degree of difficulty of the situation. When we get news about a situation that seems impossible to deal with, while others are tearing their clothes and losing hair, we ought to come forth with boldness and speak a word of declaration over our situations

When Naaman arrived at the door of Elisha, the prophet sent a servant to tell him to wash in the Jordan River seven times and his flesh would be cleansed of the leprosy, but Naaman went away wroth because he expected the prophet to come out side to him and perform some religious rituals. He almost missed his healing because he allowed anger to take control and he did not understand the power of the spoken prophetic word. How many people have missed their healing because they did not have faith in the simplicity of the prophetic word spoken from the mouth of one of God's servants? There may be times when we expect something grandiose to happen, but our breakthrough and our deliverance can come through a prophet word spoken and embraced.

Fidel Donaldson

Chapter 15

Prophetic Performance

From Barren to Bountiful

When the season of Jesus' birth came around, the Angel Gabriel visited a priest named Zacharias who had a wife named Elizabeth. This couple is described in *Luke* 1:6 as being righteous before God, walking in all the commandments and ordinances of the Lord, but they had no children because Elizabeth was barren, and they were both elderly. There are seasons in our lives when we will endeavor to walk in the fullness of the things of God and still deal with barrenness, but we must not become discouraged because a prophetic word can take us from being barren to bountiful. If you are in that season right now, do not speak about the adversary and do not allow a spirit of defeat to take over your speech. When your Kairos season comes, God will send a word of life and fruitfulness to you.

I love the fact that Zacharias continued to be faithful in his calling as priest despite the fact that his prayers had not been answered. When it was his turn to burn incense in the temple, he did not abandon his post. While he was burning the incense in the temple and the people were praying on the outside, he received an angelic visitation. When he saw Gabriel, he was in fear, so Gabriel had to calm his nerves. He instructed Zacharias that his prayer was heard and his wife Elisabeth would bear a son. In spite of the barrenness and the fact they were both well stricken in age, Zacharias continued to pray until there was an angelic manifestation. His wife Elizabeth was chosen by God to bear John the Baptist; the one who would be the forerunner of Jesus. Your situation may be barren at the present time, but please don't stop praying prophetically and speaking the word of life because your season of fruitfulness and productivity are on the way.

Dummies In the Church

After telling Zacharias all the wonderful things God would do through his son John, instead of rejoicing, Zacharias responded by saying, *"Whereby shall I know this? For I am an old man, and my wife well stricken in years" (Luke 1:18).* My brother and my sister, when you have endured seasons of barrenness and have prayed, and the season come when God sends a word, please don't allow the impossibility of your situation to cloud your mind, causing you to question what God has spoken. It does not matter how long you have been in a situation, prayer and the prophetic word can produce a breakthrough.

After explaining to Zacharias that he was Gabriel, and he stood in the presence of God and was sent by God to speak to him and to show him glad tidings, Gabriel told him, *"And, behold, thou shalt be dumb, and not able to speak, until the day that these things shall be performed, because thou believest not my words, which shall be fulfilled in their season" (Luke1:20).* Is it possible that the reason why we have dummies in the church is because God is not going to allow them to speak doubt through unbelief which will interfere with his plan to birth something through them? If we are going to pray, then we should have faith and if we are not going to exercise faith then why bother praying! He was not able to speak until the day the thing spoken by Gabriel would be performed. This is a great example of the power of the tongue to cause fruitfulness or barrenness. The Greek word for *performed* as it used there is *ginomai* and it means; *to cause to be; to become or to come into being.* A word from God spoken in faith and received by faith can cause things that are not to come to fruition. There is not a barren situation that we face that is greater than God's ability to produce fruit in our life.

The Kairos Season

Gabriel told Zacharias that the words would be fulfilled in their season. It is vitally important for us to understand that our lives in God are governed by times and seasons. *"To everything there is a season, and a time to every purpose under the heaven" (Ecclesiastes 3:1).* The word season there speaks of *an occasion, a set or proper time.* While you are waiting on your season of restoration and deliverance, don't wait in fear and doubt but wait in prayer praise and prophecy. You have the Spirit of prophecy on the inside of you, the dunamis miracle working power of God and you should not be afraid to use it. Some seasons are long, and some seasons are short, but whatever season you find yourself in, heed the words of the Apostle Paul that he spoke to the Galatians, *"And let us not be weary in well doing: for in due season we shall reap, if we faint not (Galatians 6:9).* Zacharias and his wife Elizabeth endured a long season of barrenness but he continued to be faithful in executing the priest's office and continued to pray although the barrenness was exacerbated by the fact, they were both well stricken in age. The length of time and the severity of our situation cannot negate a prophetic word from the Lord. Our Holy Bible contains a word for every situation we will face, and the Holy Spirit on the inside of us will illuminate and activate that word when it is spoken and believed by faith.

Here is something fascinating to contemplate. Six months after visiting Zacharias, the Angel Gabriel visited a young virgin named Mary. He brought her a word about a son that would be birthed through her womb. Although she was young and living in a city of Galilee named Nazareth, Gabriel's salutation to her was, *"Hail, thou that art highly favored, the Lord is with thee: blessed art thou among women"* (*Luke 1:28*). Like Zacharias, when Mary saw Gabriel she was in fear and was troubled by the salutation. Gabriel calmed her fear by telling her that she had found favor with God. Fear can grip the young like Mary, and it can grip the old like Zacharias, but whether young or old we need to understand that we have favor with God and that favor can bring a word from God that will take us from barren to bountiful.

Gabriel told her she would bring forth a son and did the same thing he did to Zacharias; He told Mary what to name the baby and of all the great things God would do with him. Instead of rejoicing, Mary asked the question, *"How shall this be, seeing I know not a man"* (*Luke 1:34*). *"And the angel answered and said unto her, The Holy Ghost shall come upon thee, and the power of the Highest shall overshadow thee: therefore also that holy thing which shall be born of thee shall be called the Son of God"* (*Luke 1:35*). Beloved know and understand this, when the Holy Ghost comes He comes with power and authority.

Man will not be able to take credit for what God is going to birth through us in the Kairos season because it will be done through the power of the Holy Spirit. The Holy Ghost and the prophetic word will make the dry places fertile. Here is the crux of the matter; Elizabeth could not get pregnant until it was in the season when Mary could conceive because Elizabeth's son was chosen by God to prepare the way for Mary's son. God will shut the womb in-order to prevent us from birthing out of season, so we must discern the times and the seasons and wait in a prophetic posture of worship and prayer until the season turns from barren to bountiful.

Be It Unto Me According to thy Word

Gabriel informed Mary that her cousin Elisabeth had conceived a son in her old age, and that was the sixth month with her that was called barren. I love the fact that prayer produced an angelic visitation and a word that put barrenness in the past. Gabriel went on to tell Mary, *"For with God nothing shall be impossible."* That statement from

Praise Worship and the Spirit of Prophecy

Gabrielle should be the disciple's mantra. There is nothing that is impossible with God. No matter the degree of difficulty of your situation; nothing shall be impossible with God!!! Mary responded to Gabriel by saying, *"Behold the handmaid of the Lord; be it unto me according to thy word. And the angel departed from her."* Gabriel did not leave Mary until she had complete trust in the word he brought from God. That statement, *"be it unto me according to thy word"* should be another mantra of the disciples. When faced with impossible or difficult trials, let the words of your mouth and the meditation of your heart be acceptable to the Lord by saying, *"be it unto me according to thy word."* Take a moment now and prophesy to your present and to your future, by saying, *"be it unto me according to thy word."*

There Shall be a Performance

Once Mary reached the point of understanding of the word spoken by Gabriel, she went with haste to a city of Juda, entered the house of Zacharias and saluted her cousin Elizabeth. Remember, Juda means praise and we should make haste to get to Juda, to get to a place of praise. As soon as Elizabeth heard Mary's salutation, the babe in her began to leap, and Elizabeth was filled with the Holy Ghost. Here is another of many confirmations concerning the Holy Spirit and prophesy. As soon as Elizabeth was filled with the Holy Ghost, she began to prophesy: *"And she spake out with a loud voice, and said, Blessed art thou among women, and blessed is the fruit of thy womb."* She did not whisper but prophesied boldly with a loud voice to confirm that which was spoken to Mary by the angel Gabriel.   The Holy Ghost will cause us to speak the word boldly and to prophesy. Elizabeth told Mary as soon as the voice of the salutation sounded in her ears, the babe leaped in her womb for joy. She told Mary she was blessed because she believed: for there shall be a performance of those things which were told her from the Lord. Belief or faith will cause blessings to come our way. We should not say we believe, and then speak words of doubt and uncertainty. If we say we believe, then we should not doubt or be double minded.

When you hear the voice of someone you are divinely connected to through what God is birthing, the babe in you will begin to leap for Joy because the time of deliverance is near. Don't allow folks into your sphere whose words will bring death to your spiritual baby. Get in the company of folks who speak words that cause your baby to leap.   The Greek word for *performance* there is *teleiosis* and it means *perfection, completion of prophecy*. God is going to perfect and complete the prophetic word He has spoken to us. Mary joined in Elizabeth's prophetic declaration by saying: *"My soul doth magnify the Lord and my spirit hath rejoiced in God my savior."* The prophetic word from the Lord will bring order, structure and clarity. When Ezekiel prophesied to the dry bones, each bone came together and was connected properly to another bone. Mary was fearful and troubled when Gabriel appeared to her, but when she received clarity and met up with Elizabeth she began to rejoice and magnify God.

Praise Worship and the Spirit of Prophecy

Please do not forget how close the word of God is; remember it is in our mouths and in ours hearts, and it is the word of faith. The same word Mary spoke when she said, *"Be it unto me according to thy word."* The same word of faith spoken by Elisabeth when she told Mary, *"blessed is she that believed: for there shall be a performance of those things which were told her from the Lord."* The same word of faith used by Elijah to stop the rain and bring the oil and meal to the widow; the same word of faith Ezekiel used to prophesy to the dry bones causing them to live; the same word of faith Jesus used when he spoke to the wind, beating against the boat and said, *"Peace be still."* You and I have the same word of faith in us and that word shall produce a performance if we do not allow fear to cripple it. Prior to Jesus rebuking the wind, the disciples were full of fear. Once He caused the wind to cease and there was great calm, He said to them, *"Why are ye so fearful? How is it that ye have no faith?"* (Mark 4:40). Wow! You mean to tell me people can be with Jesus and have no faith?

Fear will cripple the prophetic word in your belly. Do not allow the diagnosis or the negative prognosis to cripple you with fear. Do not allow the lengthy prison sentence to cause you to contemplate suicide or to keep you in a place of oppression and depression. Remember, the greater one is living on the inside of you through the Spirit, if you have been born again. If you are reading this, and you have not repented of your sins and accepted Jesus into your life as Lord and savior, please take a moment to do so now. Just pray and confess your sins before Him. Ask Him to forgive you and to come into your heart and be the Lord of your life. Ask Him to fill you with the Holy Spirit. If you are born again, make up your mind to stand on the word God has placed in you. Strengthen your relationship with the Holy Ghost and allow Him to lead your life. Wherever you are at the present time, you are God's ambassador, a man or woman with power and authority. You have the ability in the Spirit of God to transform any atmosphere or environment through worship and the prophetic word. You are God's mouthpiece or He will raise up a rock. Do not allow a rock to take your place because of fear. Do not allow the environment or the people in it to determine who you are and what you do, or to hold you hostage to your past. Always remember who you are and to whom you belong; You are a child of God endued with power from on high to have dominion and authority in earth. Step out with boldness and allow the gifts God has invested in you to come forth!

CPSIA information can be obtained
at www.ICGtesting.com
Printed in the USA
FFOW03n0721280917
40344FF